Staged to Sell (or Keep)

Easy Ways to Improve the Value of Your Home

by Jean Nayar

Copyright © 2009 Filipacchi Publishing, a division of Hachette Filipacchi Media U.S., Inc.

First published in 2009 in the United States of America by
Filipacchi Publishing
1633 Broadway
New York, NY 10019

Design: Patricia Fabricant
Editing: Lauren Kuczala
Production: Ed Barredo

ISBN 13: 978-1-933231-57-0

Library of Congress Control Number: 2008938172

Printed in the U.S.A.

Photo credits

Anthony + Masterson: 68, 105 top right. Edmund Barr: 31 right, 148 left, 153 top center. Charles Bush: 21 bottom left. Greg Campbell: 22 top, 23 right, 85 bottom, 139 top left. John Coolidge: 75. Grey Crawford: 28 bottom. Colleen Duffley: 36 top, 126. Tria Giovan: 13 bottom, 77 bottom, 84, 110-111, 153 bottom, 157 bottom right. Liz Glasgow: 26, 73 top, 136 top. Ed Gohlich: 28 top left, 63 left, 100 top right, 104, 112, 117 top. Sam Gray: 20. Gridley & Graves: 16, 18, 41, 71, 133. John Gruen: 19, 35, 45, 46 bottom, 48, 51, 78 bottom, 88 right, 89, 100 bottom, 101 bottom, 103 top right, 118 left and right, 120, 121 left, 122, 123 right, 132 top, 148 center, 149. Jamie Hadley: 17 top and bottom right, 53, 87 bottom, 124-125. Aimee Herring: 21 right, 49, 82, 88 left, 103 top left, 108-109, 119, 123 left, 129, 138 top, 139 bottom, 147, 148 right, 150, 151 top, 152, 158, 159 top left. Nancy Hill: 14-15, 38. Len Lagrua: 47 bottom. Jennifer Levy: 17 bottom left, 42 bottom, 127 bottom. David Duncan Livingston: 30, 31 top and bottom left. Mark Lohman: 27 bottom, 29, 40, 44, 47 top, 79 top, 87 top, 106 top, 116 top left and bottom, 130, 131 right, 136 bottom, 157 bottom left. Janet Mesic Mackie: 11, 12 right, 13 left and top right, 78 top. Angus McCritchie: 146, 157 top left. Virginia McDonald: 153 top right. Jeff McNamara: 4-5, 6-7, 66-67, 70 right, 90-91, 93, 100 top left, 142. Susan McWhinney: 12 bottom left, 103 bottom, 107 top and center, 132 bottom. Karyn Millet: 64-65, 85 left, 128 top, 131 left, 154 top. Keith Scott Morton: 39 bottom left and right, 69, 76, 94, 95 left, 96 top, 97, 98 left, 99 right, 106 bottom, 107 bottom, 113, 137 top right, 144 top. Matthew Millman: 83 bottom. Laura Moss: 23 left, 61, 139 top right, 151 bottom, 156 top. Michael Partenio: 42 top, 77 top, 137 top left, 137 bottom left and right, 157 top right, 159 top center and right, 159 bottom left, center and right. Erik Rank: 39 top. Rion Rizzo: 145. Eric Roth: 34, 72, 73 bottom, 121 right. Kate Roth: 28 top right, 62 right, 140-141, 153 top left, 154 bottom. Joe Schmelzer: 9, 17 top left, 24-25, 32-33, 43, 50 bottom right, 83 top, 95 right, 105 left, 128 bottom, 156 bottom right, 157 bottom right. Stan Stankiewicz: 80 bottom, 81 bottom, 98 bottom right. Tim Street-Porter: 144 bottom. Robin Stubbert: 50 top left, 59, 63 right, 116 top right, 117 bottom, 127 top. Philip Clayton Thompson: 96 bottom. Chris Vaccaro: 36 bottom, 37, 56, 79 bottom, 115, 156 bottom left. Michael Weschler: 12 top left, 50 bottom left, 52, 60, 92, 102, 155. Jim Yochum: 21 top left, 62 left, 101 top, 138 bottom.

CONTENTS

Introduction

Of all the investments you'll ever make, none is more important than your home. Whether you want to keep your house or sell it, finishing it out and furnishing it in a way that makes the most of its potential is the key to improving the value of your investment—and to extracting its full worth when it's time to sell. Either way, the possibilities for enhancing the character, function and beauty of your home—to support your own lifestyle or to enable potential buyers to see how it might bolster theirs—are vast. And this book is designed to help you sort through the options.

With many homeowners still reeling from the aftershocks of the recent mortgage crisis and concerned about inflation and a volatile economy in the future, now is the ideal time to put forth a little extra energy to protect and enhance the value of your home—whether you plan to continue to live in it, are determined to sell it this month, or want to enhance its resale value for 10 or 20 years from now. Improving certain parts of your home may demand applying substantial elbow grease or parting with a good chunk of your wallet. But the real or perceived value of other areas can often be improved with minimal effort—and without spending a cent.

Clearly organized, filled with photos of inspiring rooms and brimming with expert tips, this book shows you how to look at your home from the inside out, recognize its strengths and weaknesses, and learn how to bring out its best. You'll find expert advice on choosing or improving the surfaces of your walls, windows, ceilings and floors, as well as tips on selecting and arranging furniture to enhance the configuration of your rooms, and with it, the quality of your life. You'll also discover how to refresh and recycle existing furnishings and add function and comfort with soft furnishings such as curtains, shades, bedding and slipcovers. Plus, you'll get practical ideas and helpful hints on controlling clutter, brightening rooms with color and light, and enhancing outdoor spaces.

Best of all, the ideas presented here can be implemented in an hour, an afternoon or over several years, depending on your timeframe and your goals. And, like some of the best things in life, many of them cost very little—or are even free.

Define Your Style

Contemporary fabrics and accents in lively colors and
patterns update a collection of traditional furnishings
with a subtle, fresh twist.

An ideal home invariably means different things to different people. But the most appealing houses—whether compact country cottages or grand manors—always possess a clear sense of style. For some people, infusing a home with individual style comes as naturally as breathing. For others, sifting through a dizzying array of paints, fabrics, furnishings and fixtures can overwhelm their attempts to find their own visual voice.

Yet, in any endeavor to improve the quality of a house—particularly one you plan to keep—it's vital to home in on a visual style that not only reflects the essence of who you are but also brings out the best in the house's natural character. If you want to sell your home, clarifying its style also helps a prospective buyer see it with a cohesive view, enabling him or her to easily picture living, working, eating and sleeping in its rooms or relaxing in its yard.

To help you distill a visual point of view for your home, this chapter presents a range of interior settings, which are divided into sections depicting several general style categories and highlighting furnishings and accents that support and reflect different approaches to living. Whether you are a dyed-in-the-wool traditionalist or a committed modernist, a country girl or a dreamy romantic, designing a home to live in is about surrounding yourself with furnishings, colors, accents and art that make you happy. It's about knowing your likes and dislikes, starting with an essential foundation of furnishings, then layering in pieces over time to create an environment that reinforces your values and how you want to live.

Staging a home to sell, on the other hand, is more about putting its best face forward. To do this, you may need to edit some of your furnishings or accents—paring away highly personal pieces or those acquired willy-nilly over time—to allow a future owner to see a room's potential. In this case, developing a clear style should be more about presenting an essential template of furnishings that can enable other people to envision how they might imprint a house with their personal stamp and make it their own.

The rooms in one section may resonate with you immediately, while spaces in another might appeal to your spouse. Or you may see room settings and ideas in two or three sections that appeal to you or other family members. The trick is to look for the dominant themes that rise to the top and, particularly if you plan to stay in your home, balance the dreams of everyone who shares the house. When cultivating a style, it's also important to consider the innate character of your home and its context. You can no sooner transform a rustic cottage into a manor house by filling it with expensive antiques than you can turn a sleek urban apartment into a mountain retreat by peppering it with lodge paraphernalia. (Often, though, seasoned designers and people with a sure sense of style mix and match furnishings and accents of different styles and eras to keep traditional settings from feeling staid or contemporary spaces from feeling arid.) Instead, think about how you can nurture your house's inherent possibilities, while accepting—yet minimizing—its limitations.

It's also worthwhile to remember that improving the value of your home is not so much a goal as it is a process, especially if you plan to stay in it awhile. When you think of your home as malleable, like a stage, you'll adapt and change it thoughtfully, with an eye toward the big picture. Will you be staying put for the long haul? Or do you plan to be moving out soon? Thinking of your home as something that can constantly be added to or subtracted from can also help you manage your budget. For as any savvy clothing shopper knows, you don't necessarily have to spend a lot of money to create great style. In fact, some seasoned pros often see an inverse proportion between style and money. Keeping in mind your long- and short-term objectives will help you clarify how to allocate your time and dollars in order to make the most of your investment.

Before you begin to change any room, take the following quiz to see which style emerges as a reflection of your lifestyle preferences. Then turn to the section or sections whose spaces most closely align with your dominant style type and let the images and ideas guide your decorating choices.

The green-and-slate striped silk curtains and clean-lined neutral furnishings—set off by a pair of reupholstered armchairs—give this living room classic contemporary appeal without feeling sterile.

STYLE QUIZ

1. **Which colors are you comfortable living with in your home?**

A Deep, rich colors and—always—white trim
B Pure, light naturals with a bright accent or two
C Sunny yellows, crisp blues, brisk reds
D I'm open to most colors, as long as they suit the room and the mood I'm trying to create
E Gem tones spiced with black lacquer, a touch of gold
F Earth tones, browns, greens
G Pastels and soft colors, nothing too jarring

2. **Your perfect house would be:**

A An 18th-century townhouse in a historic neighborhood
B A mid-century style with clean lines and lots of glass
C A charming cottage with a big fireplace and a front porch swing
D An offbeat stone house or mountain retreat, with architectural features to design around, and nooks and crannies for collectibles
E A Mediterranean-style villa, with balconies and views, in southern California
F A Shingle-style house, with a comfortable family room and big yard, in a friendly neighborhood
G A restored Victorian, complete with all the original trimmings

3. **A room accessory you might choose is:**

A A high-quality globe
B A work of modern art
C A vintage sign
D A carved statue from Papua New Guinea
E A starburst mirror
F A storage ottoman
G A mosaic-topped side table

4. **What's your idea of a great evening spent with friends?**

A Dinner out, followed by a concert or play
B Going to a trendy new restaurant or wine tasting
C Playing games, chats, homemade pie in front of the fire
D Taking part in a progressive dinner, with different courses served at different homes
E Going to a great ethnic restaurant and seeing an ethnic dance performance
F Throwing a spur-of-the-moment gathering at home
G Seeing a chick flick, browsing in a bookstore, stopping for coffee at an out-of-the-way cafe

5. **What look do you prefer for a bed?**

A A fine spread, with a simple accent pillow or two, perhaps a tailored bedskirt
B Totally clean, with exposed legs and the cover tucked around the mattress
C A crisp white bedskirt topped with a quilt, preferably one made by a family member
D A handmade coverlet purchased on a trip to a foreign place
E Silks and velvets in deep colors, custom made into sleek coverlets and pillows
F Easy-care and washable coverings, not too fussy, in a pattern or color that doesn't show wear and tear
G Lots of ruffled pillows, puffy comforters and a lacy bedskirt

6. **Your personal style is best summed up as:**

A Slightly reserved and a little formal
B Crisp and clean
C Never met a stranger
D Open to new people, new places and new ideas
E Polished and tinged with mystery
F Friendly and down-to-earth
G Sometimes dreamy, always thoughtful, glass-half-full outlook

7. **The upholstery and drapery fabrics that usually catch your eye are:**

A Damasks, tapestries, tone-on-tone stripes or classic motifs, nothing trendy
B Crisp linens, fabrics that are more about texture than pattern
C Ginghams, starched curtains, nubby off-white slipcovers
D Asian-inspired fabrics with unusual colors or patterns
E Silks, soft-to-the-touch materials like suede or ultra-suede, animal prints
F Go-with-anything neutrals, simple prints or plaids
G Sheer or lacy, with cabbage-rose prints and muted, dusty tones

ANSWERS

Add up the number of times you've circled each letter for an answer. The letter you circled most indicates your dominant style; each letter corresponds to the style in the list below.

A TRADITIONAL
B MODERN
C COUNTRY
D ECLECTIC
E GLAMOROUS
F CASUAL
G ROMANTIC

TRADITIONAL

If you're drawn to old, formal houses built more than 75 to 100 years ago, then you'll probably be most comfortable with a traditional style. While the particular architectural features of a traditional home may vary, they're always rooted in the European styles of previous centuries. Some traditional houses are luxurious and refined, with formal spaces inspired by stately English manors, sophisticated French chateaux or elegant Italian palazzi. Others, such as a Colonial- or Greek Revival–style house, or a Georgian or Federal townhouse, can be understated and sometimes quite modest in scale or architectural ornamentation. The rooms in a traditional house often have symmetrical features and layouts, and will usually include crown moldings, divided-light windows, wood floors and wainscoting. Even if it is a new structure, the form of a traditional-style house will include at least intonations of European architectural styles of the past.

By the same token, if you're attracted to European or American antiques or furnishings, or to variations of these furnishings, such as updated Windsor chairs or mahogany sleigh beds, then you'll know that traditional-style furniture is best for you. Again, even if the furniture and accessories in a traditional home are new, their materials, shapes and colors will be familiar. In more refined traditional homes, you might find a few elegant Biedermeier, Louis XVI or Regency antiques; in more modest traditional settings, Chippendale or Queen Anne–inspired pieces made of walnut or mahogany are likely to prevail.

The palettes favored by traditionalists often include warm, familiar colors, such as deep reds and burgundies, soothing

Classic brick-red walls add spark to a sunroom fitted out with traditional-style furnishings. The bold tone is a strong backdrop to the overscale mirror.

olive and sage greens, and understated tans, taupes, khakis, creams and other neutrals. Sometimes, however, traditionalists will opt for bolder colors, including bright yellow or robin's-egg blue, that were popular during the Georgian or Colonial eras. Others favor tone-on-tone schemes. They typically prefer fabrics in classic patterns, such as stripes and damasks, and appreciate full-length draperies often topped with valances or pelmets.

Outside, a traditional home might be surrounded by manicured gardens, and grounds might include a pergola or gazebo. On the other hand, the trees and shrubs might be more naturalistic, like an 18th-century English landscape garden.

LEFT, TOP: Around an elegant dining table, inherited treasures, shield-back Hepplewhite side chairs along with Windsor chairs at both ends—keep a traditional setting lively. A collection of Blue Willow china complements the scene.

LEFT, BOTTOM: A vintage trunk serves as both stylish storage and a generous-size coffee table in this cozy den. A recycled table becomes the perfect perch for a hammered brass lamp and books. Inexpensive chenille toss pillows reinforce the rich, warm colors in the sofa's paisley fabric. Small touches, such as the tiny framed topiaries and ivy plant in a recycled sugar bowl that had lost its top, add to the room's inviting, reassuring good looks.

OPPOSITE: In this semiformal dining room, a Roman shade made of an abstract botanical fabric hung above a cabinet built into the bay window introduces a fresh but familiar pattern. The moss-green walls and yellow ceiling are balanced by the creamy molding. The rug grounds the room with colors and motifs echoed throughout the space.

ABOVE: The subtle floral drapery panel hung behind a classic four-poster canopy bed picks up the garden theme in this master bedroom. The French doors look onto a private porch. The walls and ceiling employ two shades of green to create a subtle visual gradation.

RIGHT, TOP: The neutral materials palette keeps the master bathroom serene. The floor is Negev limestone, bordered by rough-cut Jerusalem limestone. The tub is encased with mahogany panels to match the custom shutters. Left bare, the upper windows allow daylight to stream into the space.

RIGHT, BOTTOM: An antique console inherited from the owner's grandmother sets a traditional tone in an entrance hall in front of the staircase. A tall, dramatic lamp holds it own next to the ornate gilded mirror above the lovely piece of furniture.

MODERN

Fans of modern style might be as drawn to a house designed in the mid-20th century as they are to a condo designed in the early 21st century. As long as the setting features open spaces that flow into each other, furniture with clean lines often in asymmetrical spatial arrangements, machined materials such as chrome, Lucite, metal and smooth wood, and minimal architectural ornamentation, the modernist will feel at home.

For modernists who regard their home as a sanctuary, rooms might be understated oases of comfort and calm with subtle neutral palettes, natural fabrics and a carefully edited mix of clean-lined Danish-designed wood furnishings. For technophiles and those who love cutting-edge design, spaces might be bold, vibrant and sleek, with a brightly colored wall, a large piece of Pop Art, molded metal furnishings and roller shades made of synthetic mesh.

Either way, common threads are likely to include a minimalist mix of furnishings with simple lines, limited geometric patterns, plenty of materials rich with texture, and not an ounce of clutter. A large, flat-screen television is probably the focal point of the family room, where an Antonio Citterio table might stand next to a Hans Wegner sofa. A kitchen might feature recycled or eco-conscious materials or reclaimed wood floors, while a simple platform bed, topped by Zen-inspired organic bedding, might be the centerpiece of a bedroom.

Modern houses are often designed to harmonize with their settings, fitting in with the landscape like hand in glove. Their surroundings are often naturalistic, laced with monolithic stone benches and wrap-around terraces, enabling their inhabitants to commune with nature. The sound of a trickling fountain might soothe frayed nerves on a patio at the end of the day, the light from a single lantern might illuminate a covered terrace at night, or a simple Japanese-inspired pool house might sit at the end of a placid pool. On the other hand, modernist outdoor rooms might include chic chaises longues and ultra-hip party lights, while gardens might feature crisply clipped parterres.

Crisp white furnishings give this airy room a contemporary yet intimate feeling. Dark-stained oak floors and new grid work on the ceiling enrich the space without frills. A bronze-and-steel drum chandelier with an open configuration doesn't impede sight lines and looks like a piece of art.

Upholstered furnishings with rolled arms and soft curves bring warmth to a setting that leans modern. Mies van der Rohe's Barcelona stool stands out as a classic modern focal point.

TOP: Leather-topped barstools add a vintage flavor.

ABOVE: Mid-century modern furnishings define a playful breakfast nook.

RIGHT, TOP: Modern double-duty storage is stylish and purposeful.

RIGHT, BOTTOM: Sleek graphic art adds punch.

COUNTRY

The country/cottage-style home is all about comfort. The house might be a rustic mountain retreat, a seaside beach house, a lakeside cabin or a Cape Cod cottage. Country dwellings are typically compact, one-story structures. Outside they're often surrounded by a picket or hand-hewn fence; inside, their walls are generally covered by beaded board or pine paneling. Some, like European country houses or gentlemen's farmhouses, can be quite sophisticated and grand. Whether old or new, country houses are brimming with charm and personal style.

Furnishings in a country/cottage home might include a handful of family heirlooms or hand-me-downs mixed with tag-sale pieces or flea-market finds. Wood furnishings are often painted white or pale blue or green. Overstuffed sofas and flea-market chairs encourage family and friends to sit back and kick up their feet. Slipcovers often top

ABOVE: Vintage accents bring notes of warmth and charm to a mix of contemporary furnishings in a modern country-style room.

OPPOSITE: Graphic checks and rooster statues give this relaxed room touches of country flavor.

upholstered furniture to unify disparate pieces and keep things low-maintenance (children are always at ease in country homes). In the dining room you might find a big pine farm table or stenciled oak hutch, both weathered over time. Wall colors tend toward pastels—pale blue, pink, green or yellow, usually offset by crisp white molding. Cushions, curtains and bedding in English florals and gingham fabrics often prevail. Swedish checks and ticking stripes or French provincial toiles or paisleys can also dominate in country/cottage dwellings. Earthier tones are often seen in more rustic country houses, however, where you're likely to find tartan throws and plaid or striped seat cushions. Framed family photos in the living room might recall memories of an earlier generation, while an offbeat paint color—apple green or tomato red—on the walls of a family room might indulge the tastes of an emerging one. Bedrooms are pretty, with painted metal beds and handmade quilts. And wood floors are likely to be topped with boldly striped flat-weave or braid rugs.

Outdoors, a country/cottage house will likely feature a swing on a covered porch, picnic tables and benches in the yard, a potting shed, and border gardens with plump hydrangeas or an arbor or trellis covered with climbing roses.

OPPOSITE; ABOVE, TOP AND BOTTOM: White furniture and woodwork set off by shades of yellow, red or blue are classic ingredients in any country room recipe. Florals and checks are favorite patterns.

ABOVE: An old bench, topped with a quilt, sits at the foot of the master bed. The frame isn't vintage, but looks like it is. Leaving the windows curtainless keeps the room looking clean and enables the eye to be drawn to the sweetly patterned bedding.

ECLECTIC

If you're an adventurer who travels around the world (or to antique shops) and brings home curios—such as Moroccan poufs, Indian saris or hand-carved Puerto Rican santos—from every place you go, chances are your style is eclectic. People with eclectic style aren't driven by trends, though they're probably well aware of them, and are comfortable in any number of settings—a stone chateau or an urban loft, a Spanish Colonial–style house or a rustic lodge-like dwelling.

Living spaces will invariably include an offbeat mix of furnishings—a grandmother's Victorian sofa, reupholstered in cotton muslin, along with a pair of Eero Saarinen chairs from the 1950s, perhaps—while a master bedroom might get a shot of color with a bevy of silk cushions from Thailand atop the four-poster bed topped with mosquito netting or a swath of Indian print fabric. These spaces may include a mix of modern art with antique furniture, or they might be styled with a commingling of contemporary furniture and primitive accents from Africa or South America. Talismans from around the globe—a

Mexican milagro, perhaps, or a 19th-century Chinese Buddha statue—inject private spaces with energy and personality.

On the outdoor terrace of an eclectic home, you might find a Chinese lantern over a Tahitian teak table surrounded by Spanish chairs. The only constant in eclectic environments is the element of surprise.

OPPOSITE, TOP: In this master bedroom, the bed was designed to frame objects such as a flea-market chandelier and a sunburst mirror. The white oak nightstands look like sculptures. Crewel draperies pay homage to a Southern heritage.

OPPOSITE, BOTTOM: The Greek key pattern in the mirror frame contrasts with a Chinese-style stool.

ABOVE: In the living room, an antique wing chair is upholstered in a robin's-egg blue fabric. The terra cotta striped wallpaper provides a soothing backdrop and color cue for a large ottoman and chair covered in woven textiles with exotic motifs.

RIGHT: In this living room, a pleasing palette of warm neutrals reigns. The mirror over the fireplace is an adaptation of a Chippendale pattern. Crewel draperies and a sisal rug contrast with the dark woods and an earthy antique French armoire.

GLAMOROUS

For those who love glamorous style, a bungalow in the Hollywood Hills, a Mediterranean-inspired villa in Beverly Hills or a luxury condo in Las Vegas could all serve as home base. A palatial suburban pad in Dallas or an apartment in a midtown Manhattan high-rise could also do the trick. The key to a glamorous setting is polish.

The living room of a glamorous house might include Art Deco–inspired furnishings, a pair of white porcelain greyhounds, and a faux leopard-skin throw. In dining spaces you'd probably find an Italian crystal chandelier, a work of gutsy modern art and a mirrored console. The glamorous bedroom is the ultimate retreat, with gauzy floor-length curtains, a shapely upholstered headboard, silk or satin bedding, a Garbo-worthy vanity and an upholstered chaise. To get a picture of contemporary glamorous style, think of the interiors designed by Jamie Drake or Kelly Wearstler. Even a child's room will have a touch of glamour—imagine framed vintage French posters, lacquered furniture, hot pink walls and a glorious canopy over the bed.

ABOVE: In this fanciful foyer, the openwork patterns of the pillows and mirrors contrast with walls adorned with wallpaper flocked with bird motifs.

RIGHT: A zebra rug sets off the graphic vine print wallpaper in this lively work space.

Rooms in glamorous houses are likely to have glass doors that open onto terraces or patios that may look onto a pool. Comfy lounge chairs surrounding the pool might be separated by well-manicured potted fruit trees. Lush flowering hibiscus and bougainvillea bring color to the surroundings and scent the air.

ABOVE: Topped with an overscale sunburst mirror, a glamorous vintage headboard reupholstered in linen and highlighted with nail heads commands attention in this upbeat bedroom.

RIGHT: Painted muslin-gray, the ceiling warms up this zesty dining room and harmonizes with the charcoal walls. Graphic black-and-white patterns on the rug and curtains add energy, and white urns and statuary inject wit.

Cozy chenille fabrics make the sofa and loveseat in this relaxed family room warm and inviting. Classic checked shades contrast with crisp framed photos.

OPPOSITE: Cheerful touches of yellow liven up a spacious white kitchen. Caramel-colored oak floors add an extra shot of warmth to the space. Pendant lights reminiscent of fishermen's lanterns provide a casual air.

CASUAL

Nothing puts no-frills people at ease like a casual-style home. It might be an American ranch-style house or a Prairie foursquare. It could be a suburban tract or a Santa Fe pueblo-style home. It could also be a Shaker house or a Shingle house, or even a Cape Cod, Chicago or California bungalow. Usually casual houses have simple, efficient or informal floor plans, and little exterior or interior ornamentation. Simplicity is the key to these houses—and they're often extremely well crafted.

Some people with casual style are very selective about what they bring into their homes and will only settle for well-made furniture with pure lines, such as Shaker- or Mission-style pieces. They also like pure natural materials, such as weathered wood floors, stone countertops, and cotton or wool fabrics. Other people with casual style are less concerned with character and materials, and more concerned about comfort and ease of maintenance. For these people, easy-care floor surfaces, hard-to-stain countertops and durable cabinets are preferred. They also like large comfy sofas and chairs upholstered in stain-resistant or forgiving fabrics, such as micro-suede or chenille. Storage spaces—from computer armoires to bookshelves to window seats with pull-out drawers—abound in every room, keeping the whole house clutter-free. Basic Roman shades in solid or simple-patterned fabrics add privacy and control light in bedrooms and baths.

Accents might include a single ceramic vase on a mantel or a beautiful simply framed mirror in a foyer.

The landscape around a casual house might include low-fuss plants to keep yard work to a minimum, as well as informal stepping-stone pathways that lead from the house to a garage or potting shed.

TOP, LEFT: Preexisting shutters were painted bright green to give this little sitting room a happy feeling.

TOP, RIGHT: Whitewashed floors, a comfy sofa and primary colors add up to a family-friendly room.

RIGHT: Painted board walls envelop a casual bed of woven natural reeds.

OPPOSITE: A quartet of sailboat prints adds a focal point to the living room's two-story-high wall. A red, white and blue color scheme and playful prints give the setting relaxed, all-American appeal.

ROMANTIC

Lovers of romantic style are practically polar opposites of those who favor casual style. While both may cherish craftsmanship, romantics like fanciful lines, richly carved woodwork, or ornate iron or grillwork. They might live in a Victorian farmhouse with gingerbread details, an Alpine chalet with heavy timber ceiling beams and stone fireplaces, or a Tudor-style, Gothic Revival or Art Nouveau–inspired house with rich architectural details. A stone French farmhouse could also serve as an ideal setting for expressing romantic style.

ABOVE: English florals, rattan accent pieces, a whimsical birdcage and decorative tiles infuse this airy living room with easy romance.

OPPOSITE, TOP LEFT: A vintage settee beneath an Austrian shade edged with ball fringe provides an appealing perch for a cup of afternoon tea.

OPPOSITE, BOTTOM LEFT: Mosaic tiles atop a wrought-iron table bring an artsy touch to a dreamy porch.

OPPOSITE, RIGHT: Ruffled bedding and an ornate dressing table give this bedroom feminine flavor.

Furnishings in the romantic-style house might range from delicate wrought-iron patio chairs to an antique fauteuil. In an entrance hall you might find a curvaceous console; in the dining room a curlicue or crystal chandelier. In the bedroom, a painted metal bed is likely to be topped with satin sheets, fluffy bedding and a plethora of pillows covered in lace-edged or embroidered shams. Upholstered pieces and windows might be covered with fabrics in toile or English floral prints, and walls might be covered with textured plasterwork, a hand-painted mural or a reproduction Colefax and Fowler wallpaper.

Outside on the patio of a romantic-style home, you might see a mosaic-topped table and bistro chairs, surrounded by pots of bright flowers. Or the floor of an outdoor balcony might be covered with decorative tiles and its edge might be rimmed with ornate iron grillwork. A collection of Victorian birdcages might sit on the windowsill of a sunroom filled with wicker chairs and chinoiserie.

Surfaces

Textured wallpaper mounted around the perimeter below the ceiling offers a twist on crown molding, adding warmth and interest to this cozy room.

ON THE WALLS

Over time, small cracks can appear in walls due to the structural settling of your home or to the material contractions and expansions that occur during natural seasonal variations in temperature. Such cracks in the concrete walls of a home's foundation or basement not only can cause cracks in plaster or drywall in rooms on the upper levels of your house, they can also create leaks that can further damage your home. If you see these kinds of problems, or if you find that doors aren't closing properly, call a professional from a company such as The Crack Team, which has franchises throughout the United States. They can affordably repair cracks in concrete by pumping in a resin material that cures into a gasket-like sealant that permanently waterproofs the crack. Whether you want to sell or keep your home, always start by repairing any cracks in your foundation or basement walls before moving on to more cosmetic improvements.

Color: Freshen Up with Paint

One of the quickest—and least expensive—ways to give a room a fresh new look and feel is by painting the walls. Walls are a room's single largest element, the "frame" for the decorative picture you create with fabrics and furnishings. Fortunately, painting walls is a manageable project for most DIYers. If you plan to sell your home, stick to neutrals, such as white, ecru, ivory or beige, or soft classic hues with broad appeal, such as light grey-blue, tan or taupe. If you're keeping your home, go ahead and paint the walls any hue that appeals to you.

HOW MUCH TO BUY?

Before you begin, figure out how much primer and paint you'll have to buy. You'll need approximately one gallon of paint to cover 350 square feet of wall surface. You can calculate the amount by multiplying wall height by width, and subtracting the measurements of open spaces like windows and doorways.

   Along with the room's size, the color you're painting over will determine how much paint to buy. If you're painting over a similar shade, you may need just one coat. If you're painting a light color over a dark one, or dark over light, you may need two or three. Prepare dark walls with a tinted primer for the best coverage.

ABOVE: A rich terra cotta hue warms the walls of the Boston townhouse of designers Ray Ehscheid and Saverio Mancina. The area rug and the ornate mirror above the marble fireplace, which is original to the home, are inexpensive finds from a home-goods store and add even more warmth to the cozy space.

OPPOSITE: A cheery, soothing blue brightens the walls of a breakfast nook. Soft furnishings in richer variations of the hue reinforce the scheme.

WHICH TYPE OF PAINT TO CHOOSE?

Oil alkyds, once the only option, have been mostly phased out in interior paints. The high gloss and durability once associated only with oils is now available in water-based latex enamels. Plus, oils emit high levels of VOCs (volatile organic compounds). These gases, which are released by the paint as it dries, can cause long-term heath problems, have an impact on global warming, give off a stronger odor and are difficult to clean up. These days, oil-based paints are primarily used for exterior projects.

Latex paints are water-based formulations with acrylic binders. There is actually no latex used in latex paints. Those made with 100-percent acrylic binders are preferred to vinyl acrylics for their better durability. This type of paint is the most common; it's easy to work with for walls and trim as well as smaller projects, like furniture. Latex paints are also easy to clean up.

Many major paint companies are now offering eco-friendly products. This means they are low- or no-VOC products that are better for your lungs as well as the ozone. These paints are formulated to be as durable and washable as regular latex paints and can be used for any project.

PRIMERS

The time-challenged will be happy to know that the quality of most paints today means that prepping walls with a coat or two of primer is often not necessary. If you are painting over paint, especially a similar color, you should get uniform coverage and good adhesion without priming. However, most experts will tell you the success of any paint job depends on the preparation of the surface. Be sure it is clean and smooth for the best results. Painting unprimed drywall or wood will result in shoddy coverage, as the paint will soak into the surface. Porous or slippery surfaces such as metal, tile and glass, as well as stained surfaces, will all benefit from a coat of primer.

CHOOSING A PALETTE

If you're planning to sell your home, when it comes to choosing a color palette, your option is simple: Paint all the walls one neutral hue, such as ecru or ivory, or slightly different shades of the same neutral hue. In a home you plan to keep, your options for choosing a palette are virtually limitless. To select the right colors for your home, it helps to remember your style and select shades that work well with the overall ambience you're aiming for. But even the most traditional rooms can benefit from a fresh approach—for example, using a cherry red in a library space instead of burgundy, or a spring green rather than hunter or sage in a dining room.

One way to start is to use something you love or already own, such as a pillow fabric swatch or a work of art, to inspire your scheme. Some paint companies offer predetermined harmonious palettes that can help guide your choices, and most have websites with tools that allow you to visualize the effect of different colors in a room. You can also collect color samples from the paint store to help you discover which color combinations you like. Move the chips around until you find pairs or groups that please you. Keep in mind that when two complementary colors, such as blue and orange, are juxtaposed, the intensity of each will heighten. And remember that virtually every color will look more intense on the wall than it does on the paint chip.

For a stimulating atmosphere, some designers suggest creating a healthy tension in a room, which you can do by choosing a paint color that contrasts with your furniture upholstery. For a soothing ambience, consider using patterns in analogous color schemes. Analogous palettes are limited to two or three adjacent hues on the color wheel, such as a mango hue and coral red.

Your best bet is to try a color before you commit. Many paint lines now make sample-size containers of colors so you can paint a test patch on a wall or a piece of posterboard. It will help you see how the color looks in various lights and how it works with what's already in the room. Also, don't ignore your surroundings. Take a walk outside to gain inspiration from nature, especially from flowers.

Be aware of color trends, without necessarily letting them dictate your choices. If you've got your heart set on this year's trendy color, consider using the hue on a single accent wall or in a small room. It will be simpler to change when you tire of it next year or next season. And bear in mind the emotional impact of color; find a hue that the whole family can appreciate in rooms that are shared. Keep in mind, too, that warm colors tend to advance and can make large rooms look cozier, while cool colors recede and can make

TOP: Balanced with white trim and furnishings, the sunny yellow walls of this room establish a lively atmosphere.

BOTTOM: In this master bedroom, hydrangea-blue walls set a soothing tone.

OPPOSITE, TOP: Painting public rooms red is an ideal way to give them energy, add drama and invite socializing and activity.

OPPOSITE, BOTTOM: A fresh green hue in a bath elicits a clean, serene ambience.

a small room look more expansive. Consider the following expert advice on the effect of some of the most popular hues:

Yellow This sunny hue is the color of a creative individual and indicates a yearning for the new and the modern. Use it when you want to nurture a sense of freedom. It's also a good choice for big spaces since it's so forgiving. Yellows can be pale and buttery, rich and spicy, or bright and citrus-y. Balance stronger yellows with neutrals, such as black, dark browns or white, so they're not overpowering. Lighter tints will lift a space and give it warmth, while golden yellows provide a glowing quality. Encouraging a social atmosphere, yellow works well in kitchens, kids' rooms, dining rooms and dens. Stronger hues appear more contemporary, while golden tones feel traditional. While yellow enhances rooms flooded with natural light, the color also helps add radiance to those that are dimmer.

Blue For a calm, harmonious setting, blue is ideal. This serene color creates a calming spirit, combats tension and supports relaxation. Deep shades lend sophistication, while grayish blues work well with aged woods. Bright mid-tone blues are perfect in fresh, upbeat spaces. Light aquas are ideal for bedrooms and spa areas. Combine blue with brown for a polished look. For nautical themes, add touches of white and red, or combine blue with yellow for a French country look. It's great for bathrooms in coastal or beach houses because it echoes the sky and water. It has a lot of depth and is the most atmospheric color in the spectrum.

Red Small rooms can benefit from a dramatic use of color, and saturated red walls make a dramatic first impression. But vivid, hot colors like red need to be balanced with other shades to soften their sting. Use reds in kitchens to convey the feeling of a cozy restaurant, or in a den to add a rustic touch. Earthy reds convey a grounded feeling, brighter shades impart a contemporary feel and coppery reds lend drama. Lighter peachy-reds add softness, and mid-tone corals offer clean modernity. Rich red shades lend themselves to active settings that promote movement and excitement. Use of this color creates a fun atmosphere and invites friendliness. We recommend offsetting rich red walls with light flooring to bounce light back into the space.

Green, a hue that merges the warmth of yellow with the coolness of blue, is the color of serenity. It enhances concentration, nurtures relationships and provides a refreshing atmosphere. In sunny environments, consider using bright shades of spring or apple green, which won't look washed-out in the sunlight. In grayer climes, you might go for two shades of green, such as peppermint-gray, to complement the soft gray light that filters in. Light greens work well in bathrooms and bedrooms, deeper versions are best in family rooms, while mint-green shades are ideal for kitchens. The stronger the color, the more it appears as a youthful and modern tone. The softer the color, the more soothing and natural. Use pastel greens in areas where there is little light. Light and mid-tones combined with brown lend a natural feeling. Green mixed with pinks and violets creates a gardenlike setting.

COLOR DOS AND DON'TS

Do think about how you use your space and what mood you want to convey, but work with colors you love. Let something you already have, such as a favorite rug, work of art or glass vase, or something you plan to purchase, such as a new upholstery or curtain fabric, serve as a starting point for inspiration.

Don't be afraid to express yourself. Color evokes emotion, therefore it can define the mood of a room. Envision colors along with places you love or that make you happy.

Do embrace the new neutrals. In addition to brighter colors, there is a strong trend toward the gray palette. In warm, cool, light or dark shades, gray is versatile yet neutral enough to be paired with a variety of bold colors.

Don't hesitate to mix it up. Choose a palette of two or even three colors. Small doses of an accent color allow you to add visual interest without overpowering the room.

Do consider the flow from one room to another. Each space in your home can have its own color scheme, but it should be integrated smoothly. You can link a bold yellow room to an adjoining room in a different color by painting the trim in both spaces a crisp white, which provides a common link.

Don't take paint colors at face value. Different qualities of light cause changes in any color. Test how the color appears in various types of natural and artificial light.

Do take a risk. A bold paint color, when used the right way, can result in a chic personal statement. One way to use a bright pink, or any bright color, for that matter, without overpowering your space is to use it sparingly, such as on one wall or the back of shelves. Or if you want to tone it down a bit, try pairing it with natural materials, such as dark wood or stone.

FINISHES

Matte or flat Durable and great for low-traffic areas, paints with non-reflective flat finishes also conceal surface imperfections. It's traditionally used on ceilings.

Eggshell Scrubbable and smooth with a soft sheen, paints with eggshell finishes are a good choice for most rooms.

Satin Even more scrubbable than eggshell, satins have a subtly glossy finish and are a good choice for high-traffic and humid areas.

Semi-gloss Used on trim, woodwork, and in children's rooms and bathrooms, durable semi-gloss paints will stand up to moisture and daily wear and tear.

High gloss A great choice for trim, moldings, cabinets and doors, easy-to-wash high-gloss paints offer a shiny finish.

FAUX FINISHES

If you plan to keep your home, consider using faux finishes to add character to often overlooked areas. If you're handy and creative, there are several faux finish kits on the market that can allow you to achieve simple sponged, mottled, glazed and combed surfaces yourself. But for murals, trompe l'oeil, strié, Venetian plaster and other more sophisticated techniques, invest in the skills of a professional.

Faux-finished walls can create pleasing backdrops in any room—particularly if your style is romantic or traditional—but certain areas can benefit from added decorative detail. Ancillary spaces, such as powder rooms, halls or stairwells, are often ideal canvases for creative expression. To add visual punch beyond paint or wallcovering, consider the use of the following hand-painted decorative techniques to reveal the hidden potential of these out-of-the-way walls, turning bland surfaces into visual spectacles.

Stylized mural and strié glazing Walls treated with a strié-glazing technique create the backdrop for a random pattern of hand-painted cherry blossoms in this powder room *(below)*. The

mural, a stylized filigree of flowers that climbs up two adjoining walls, was inspired by the cherry blossoms on the surface of a Japanese vase. The strié glazing, with its blue-gray hue, gives added dimension to the romantic landscape.

Decoupage faux bois Long used to transform walls and floors, the classic decorative technique known as faux bois approximates the look of inlaid wood marquetry with hand painting. A variation of this technique was used to tame the soaring wall framing this staircase *(right)*. Applied like decoupage cutouts, squares of hand-painted faux-bois wallcovering that copies the look of maple alternate with squares that feature leaf patterns on a simulated satinwood background. The portable panels did not require on-site hand painting.

Trompe l'oeil Though it appears to be a grand entrance, few visitors would guess this staircase *(below)* was once a service-stair eyesore. Through the trompe l'oeil artistry of a decorative painter, each surface comes alive with newfound depth and detail. The staircase's risers were originally covered with black linoleum and the balustrade made of cast iron. The artist started by painting both to look like wood. For panels framing the stairs, he created trompe l'oeil panels that look like carved oak featuring acanthus leaf details. On the stair landing, a trompe l'oeil pediment adds classical grace and scale above the window, while paint and joint compound applied to the walls create the look of textured limestone blocks.

On another landing *(below, right)*, he created what he calls "faux furniture" by constructing a vented cover for a radiator from boards and painting them to look like fine cabinetry. It rests upon a linoleum floor treated to the illusion of wood parquetry as well.

ABOVE: A faux bois decoupage technique enriches the tall walls surrounding a grand staircase.

FAR LEFT AND LEFT: Exceptional trompe l'oeil imagery creates a sense of grandeur in a service staircase. The cover over the radiator is made of plywood painted to look like fine furniture.

OPPOSITE: A stylized mural with strié glazing brings an enchanting quality to a tiny powder room.

Pattern: Consider the Potential of Wallcoverings

Wallpaper is one of the best ways to add energy to a room with pattern. But since everyone's taste in pattern, not to mention color, is so personal, you'll probably want to avoid installing it unless you plan to keep your home (except perhaps in small spaces, such as powder rooms or closets, which can benefit from a surprising note of pattern). Wallpaper can range from around $25 to up to several hundred dollars a roll, it can be tricky to install, and the adhesives of many wallpapers make them very difficult to remove. So if you plan to sell your home, spare yourself the expense and a potential buyer the grief of removing a wallpaper he or she may loathe.

If you're keeping your home, however, and you have a passion for pattern, then go for it. You can start out slowly and safely by choosing a paper with an adhesive that's easy to remove. Companies such as York, Thibaut, Seabrook and Waverly offer affordable options in a wide range of styles. You might also opt to create a focal point by papering just one wall, or create the effect of a pair of murals by framing two tall bands of wallpaper and mounting them on the wall.

CHOOSING AND MIXING PATTERNS

As with paint, choose a pattern in keeping with the style you aim to create. Designer Jamie Drake suggests that when you mix wallpaper and fabric patterns, you should vary the scale and type of patterns for a coordinated look that is pleasing to the eye. For example, select one small stripe, one big bold stripe, add a check, then a floral. A common color that reappears throughout each print or pattern will tie the wallpaper and textiles together, and the different sizes of the patterns will ensure success.

If you are concerned about making a mistake when it comes to mixing patterns, many companies offer coordinated collections. They most often can be found at fabric, paint and wallpaper stores. But Drake feels that these can be "over-coordinated" and can lack a certain spontaneity that offers true charm. The most appealing mix-and-match combinations are the ones that express your personal taste and therefore will be unique to your home.

BUYING, PREPPING AND INSTALLING WALLPAPER

Before you purchase any wallpaper, measure the height and width of the space you wish to cover (excluding any baseboards, windows, doors and moldings) and round off to the next highest foot or foot and a half. Then ask your wallpaper retailer to calculate the amount you need in your choice of print. The dimensions and the amount of wallpaper on a roll (also called a spool) vary with different manufacturers. For patterned paper, the dimensions of the repeat—the size of one complete pattern—will also affect how much you'll need to buy in order to have enough to match patterns.

Another thing to find out about the wallpaper is whether it is pre-pasted or not. If it isn't, you'll need to get the correct kind of paste to mount it on the wall. Remember that wallpaper can be extremely difficult to remove, so if you're at all uncertain about how long you want to live with it, choose a paper with an easy-to-remove adhesive. Your retailer can advise you of your options.

Before you start papering, properly prep your walls, or every nick, ding and hole will show. Be sure to remove any old, existing wallpaper or scrape off peeling paint. Remove curtain hardware, switch plates and outlet covers, repair any cracks or holes, and sand down high-gloss painted finishes to create a surface to which the paste can adhere. Finally, wash off any dirt and grime, and let the surfaces dry before papering.

Unless you feel completely comfortable, avoid installing wallpaper yourself. Consult with your retailer for recommended paperhangers or visit the website of the National Guild of Professional Paperhangers at *ngpp.org* for a list of professionals in your area.

OPPOSITE, TOP: In a sitting room, awning-stripe wallpaper in yellow and white accentuates the ceiling lines. The sofa's bold red stripes add a splash of contrasting color and complementary pattern.

OPPOSITE, BOTTOM: An upstairs bedroom follows the color scheme used in the main living space of this home—primary colors. Here, white woodwork sets off blue and red fabrics. The blue floral wallpaper above the paneled wainscoting visually raises the height of the compact room. Blue glass knobs are an old-fashioned touch on the built-in chest of drawers.

BELOW: A central panel of textured wallpaper calls attention to the bed as the focal point. Square panels wrapped in faux suede soften sound and envelop the room with a sense of warmth and comfort.

ABOVE: **A moderately priced tile laid in a brickwork pattern brings practical, down-to-earth character to an affordably spruced-up kitchen.**

BELOW: **An artful backsplash is made up of five different colored glass tiles, adding a playful note to a very personal kitchen.**

OPPOSITE, TOP: **Cool blue glass tiles accented with skinny rectangular tiles combine practicality with beauty in a modern kitchen.**

OPPOSITE, BOTTOM: **Trimmed with black accent tiles, classic subway tiles brighten a vintage kitchen with a surface that will stand the stylistic test of time.**

Texture: Add Substance and Dimension with Tile

Tile is a great way to add value to your home—particularly in kitchens and baths—whether you plan to sell or keep it. But like color and pattern, materials choices can be extremely personal, and some tiles, such as marble, can be very costly. So if you plan to sell and you're willing to upgrade your tile surfaces before you do, consider using a universally appealing and affordable tile, such as white subway tile, to freshen up these rooms affordably.

TYPES OF TILE

Tiles are made in a wide range of materials—from various stones and marbles to glass and glazed porcelain to ceramic and terra cotta. They also come in a wide range of sizes, from tiny mosaic smalti to massive slabs. They can be machine- or hand-painted with ornate patterns, glazed in various colors and crackle finishes, pressed or handmade with relief motifs, or have polished or honed surfaces. Tiles can be mixed and matched and combined in all manner of contrasting compositions. And they come in various shapes: round, oval, square, rectangular and octagonal, and even irregular shapes. As a result, tile is an extremely versatile decorative tool.

WHAT DOES TILE COST?

Along with the broad range in styles of tile comes an almost equally diverse range in price. Tile can start anywhere from a couple of dollars per square foot for basic white glazed ceramic wall tiles to $60 or more per square foot for a custom mosaic and up to several hundred dollars per square foot for rare marbles and stones. Installation costs vary depending on region, but count on about $4 to $6 per square foot on top of the cost of ceramic tile and $7 to $8 per square foot for stone tile. If you're installing tile in a home you plan to keep but still need to stick to a budget, one way to get that handmade tile of your dreams without breaking the bank is to mix a few accent pieces of handmade tile with inexpensive factory-run tile. Before investing in any tile, be sure you're choosing one that suits your purpose. Tiles come in various grades of durability suitable for wall or floor surfaces and have different levels of density and porosity, which affect how much they'll absorb or resist stains.

CLEANING AND RESURFACING TILE AND GROUT

If you want to sell your home and you've got cracked or chipped tiles and dirty grout in your kitchen or bath, you can often improve or transform their appearance by carefully cleaning or resurfacing them. If your grout was white, you can clean it easily. Start with the least acidic cleaning solution, like vinegar or baking soda mixed with water. Move on to harsher chemical cleaners, such as Mr. Clean or Lysol, if the stain is difficult to remove. If these don't completely clean your grout, try a commercial tile and grout cleaner, or use stronger products, such as oxygen bleach powder, hydrogen peroxide or chlorine bleach. These products should be well diluted before use. As a last resort, you can contact a professional tile repair service to remove the old grout and add new grout. If you have damaged stone, try using a professional service, such as Hartzstone, to restore, resurface, polish and reseal the tile. For glazed or ceramic tiles, other companies offer refinishing and reglazing services to brighten the look. The term reglazing is actually a misnomer, however, as the only way a glaze can be adhered to a tile is by firing it in a kiln. The process actually involves applying an acrylic coating over the tiles and the grout that freshens their appearance. Although the durable coating is not permanent, it can last up to 20 years and so provides an affordable way to improve dingy tile surfaces without a costly renovation.

REMOVAL AND INSTALLATION

The only way to get a permanent upgrade for broken or damaged tile is to remove it and start over. You can find tips on removing and installing tile yourself on websites such as PointClickHome.com or AsktheBuilder.com. But the work is grueling, difficult and dirty, so your best bet is to hire a pro. For more information on tile and tile professionals, visit the Tile Council of North America's website at *tileusa.com* or the National Tile Contractors Association at *tile-assn.com*.

ALL ABOUT WINDOWS

Windows add character to a house, both inside and out. The right window can brighten an undistinguished entryway or bring a beautiful garden indoors. But just as a window should suit the style of your home, it should also be made of materials that match your climate and energy needs. Whether you plan to sell your home or stay in it, the windows play a strong role in the real and perceived value of the home. With energy costs escalating, choosing windows with insulated glazing or UV-resistant coatings can make a house more comfortable and keep it operating more efficiently and cost-effectively, too.

Choosing Windows

If you're replacing windows for an old house or buying them for a new one with a traditional look, consider style and character but don't stay married to the size of the original windows. Just be sure to unify the look by keeping window grilles and trim standard. Most window companies now offer grille patterns in the standard Colonial grid as well as a wide variety of other patterns, from Victorian to Prairie style.

Location, Location, Location

The main purpose of a window is to let in light, air and the view, but the style and size should depend on its location in your home. If you plan to replace a window, keep in mind use of the room, whether it gets strong sunlight and whether privacy is an issue. If the window is to be a focal point in a large, formal space, consider a grand Palladian window. In a bathroom or anywhere natural light is vital but privacy is too, consider skylights or clerestory windows set high in a wall, which will let in the sun but block views. A bay or bow window will frame a stellar view and bring the outside in.

Since decorative windows, such as picture windows, are often fixed, operable double-hung or swinging casement windows on either side add ventilation. Casements open outward when a crank is turned. Because they're easy to open from across a sink or counter, casement windows are a good choice for kitchens, but they can block exterior space near a walkway or patio when they are open.

ABOVE: Divided-light French doors give an oceanside California home East Coast flavor.

OPPOSITE: Topped with transoms, divided-light casement windows let plenty of air and light into a cheery breakfast nook.

Getting Framed

Window frames come in several materials, each with its benefits and drawbacks. The frame's main function is to keep moisture and drafts out, but looks count, too.

Aluminum frames are lightweight, low-maintenance and less expensive than wood. Aluminum readily conducts heat, so these frames can be less energy efficient, though more expensive styles come with a layer of insulation. Since salt water causes it to rust or corrode, aluminum isn't suited to coastal areas.

Vinyl-frame windows, constructed of a plastic called PVC (polyvinyl chloride), are noncorrosive and resistant to moisture, and they have insulating properties similar to wood. The range of looks for vinyl is more limited, as the frames can't be painted and are only available in white or beige.

Wood frames are attractive, traditional and have excellent insulating properties. They are also easy to customize. The downside is that the exterior must be repainted or stained periodically to stave off rot. Clad wood frames solve this problem with a vinyl or aluminum coating that protects the exterior half of the frame. Wood is the most expensive type of frame.

Composite frames are made of compressed wood particles or fiberglass and can be painted or stained like wood frames, but they are more durable, resistant to rot and provide excellent insulation. They're also more costly than vinyl and aluminum frames.

PRICE CHECK

Size, upgrades, energy efficiency, add-ons like grilles or inset screens can bump up price.

GOOD $85 to $250 Expect fixed or double-hung windows in standard sizes with aluminum or vinyl frames and single or double panes.

BETTER $250 to $425 Selections broaden to include casement-style windows, as well as a few wood-clad options at the upper end of the price range.

BEST $425 and up Find double- and triple-pane windows with special grilles and a host of other features, such as premium-wood frames, in any style you can dream up.

Keep the Outside Out

Glass is a poor insulator. In the cold north, warm air can leak out through windows, accounting for as much as 60 to 70 percent of a home's energy loss. In warm climates, the sun streams in to heat rooms. The good news is that manufacturers now provide a range of options to address these issues.

Some windows now have two or even three panes of glass. Argon or krypton gas between panes slows the passage of warm air, making these windows ideal for cold climates. Double-paned windows with special low-emissivity (or low-E) transparent metallic coatings reduce heat flow through a window. A window with coating on the exterior pane keeps the sun's heat out, while a coating on the interior pane keeps warmed air in. In warm climates, tinted glass or reflective glass reduces incoming solar radiation.

The most energy-efficient window is the one designed for your climate. Be sure to look for Energy Star labels, which have a map that shows whether a window is considered energy efficient for your area.

The Energy Information Administration predicts substantial increases in the price of heating oil, natural gas and electricity in the future, so many homeowners are looking at window replacement as a way to save money over the long haul. A cheaper, simpler upgrade is to seal windows, doors and other gaps with acrylic caulk and weatherstripping, which can save energy and reduce utility bills. If you plan to keep your home and you replace single-pane glass windows with Energy Star–qualified products, you may be able to save a few hundred dollars on energy costs annually.

TOP: Window manufacturers now make energy-efficient replacement windows that suit historic residential structures and enable owners to lower energy bills.

BOTTOM: Large windows permit access to views, but framing them with curtains provides a layer of insulation and privacy at night.

ENERGY-SAVING TIPS

1. **Check out the doors.** If a door does not close properly or lets in a draft, you'll pay the price in utility bills. Homeowners should check the weatherstripping and any gaps around the door that can let heat escape. If these features cannot be easily fixed, it may be time to replace the door.

2. **Choose the right materials.** Vinyl window frames reduce heat transfer and will help better insulate the home. They represent 65 percent of the window replacement market.

3. **Rethink the garage.** The garage is one of the largest entry points of the home and its temperature affects the overall temperature of your home. Be sure your garage door fits properly and make sure the door that leads from the garage into the home is also energy efficient.

4. **Consider the long-term.** Many local utilities offer rebates for purchasing Energy Star–qualified windows and doors. To find available rebates or incentives, visit Energy Star's Rebate Finder at *energystar.gov*.

Shutters

If you want an alternative to curtains, draperies, shades or blinds, interior shutters are a fresh, attractive option. Interior shutters can regulate light; insulate against heat, cold and noise; and provide optimum privacy. For the allergy prone, they can be easier to clean than fabric window treatments. They can also add value to your home. Here's what you need to know to choose the perfect shutters.

STYLES

Most interior shutters have horizontal louvers (also called slats, fins or blades) that can be adjusted up and down with a vertical tilt rod to let varying amounts of light into a room.

Traditional shutters have wedge-shaped louvers, from 1¼ to 1¾ inches wide. Where the climate is colder, their small openings are more desirable. Because they're shallow, they can be mounted inside a window frame.

Plantation shutters have wider (usually from 2½ to 4½ inches), elliptical-shaped louvers. The style is suited to warmer climates as the wider slats let in more air while blocking hot sunlight. The wider slats make a more dramatic architectural statement. Though 3½-inch louvers are the most common choice, custom designs allow for narrower or wider widths.

Panel shutters have no louvers. They often have molding-like trim and can feature decorative cutouts, such as a moon or star. In order to let light into a room, the shutters themselves must be opened, though some panel shutters come in a split design with louvers on the top or bottom half.

MATERIALS

Wood shutters most often are made of basswood, a lightweight hardwood with a consistent color and a tight grain that naturally resists moisture and takes stain or paint well. Engineered wood shutters are made of wood strands and fibers that are bonded together to produce a composite unit both stronger and stiffer than natural wood. They come prefinished and have either a smooth or wood-grain finish.

Polywood is another alternative to natural wood; it's made of recyclable synthetics that are engineered and reinforced to be strong and stable. They are highly energy efficient; because the surface is baked-on, it is durable. They come in standard white and off-white tones or can be custom painted.

Vinyl shutters are lightweight and work well in a moist or damp setting because they will not warp. They cannot be painted or stained, but come prefinished in a range of popular neutrals—primarily white and off-white tones. Available mainly in plantation styles, vinyl shutters are usually the least expensive choice and make a great budget option.

ABOVE: **Simple white-painted wood shutters give the living room of a coastal cottage a clean look and give the homeowners an easy way to control ocean breezes and sunlight.**

BELOW, FROM LEFT TO RIGHT: **Shutters come in a range of shapes and sizes. The movable louvers on the semicircle top can be painted and come ready to mount; the vinyl plantation-style shutter is lightweight and low-maintenance—its 4½-inch-wide louvers let in lots of light; panel shutters often feature decorative cutouts, such as a moon, sail or star, and can be painted any color; these traditional wood shutters feature 1¼-inch louvers—multiple panels can be hinged together to best fit the window opening; these plantation shutters are moisture-resistant, recyclable and extremely energy efficient.**

ABOVE: **Painting the pine paneling in this mid-century home white enabled the owner to update the look while preserving the warmth and character afforded by the panels.**

OPPOSITE: **Wrapping the entrance foyer of this new home in white wainscoting that rises to plate-rail height gives the space classic traditional appeal.**

MILLWORK, MOLDING, CABINETS AND COUNTERS

Architectural elements such as wainscoting, wall paneling, molding, and built-in shelves and cabinets not only enrich a room with warmth and character, they can also add function. A simple chair rail protects a dining room wall from nicks and scratches, a plate rail can humanize the scale of a room with a tall ceiling, built-in bookshelves flanking a fireplace provide an extra layer of storage, raised-panel cabinets conceal pots and pans in a kitchen or toiletries in the bath.

Such character-building extras can enrich rooms lacking in personality and make a home you're trying to sell more appealing. They can also cozy up a home you want to keep with beautiful form and smart function.

Material Matters: Millwork and Molding

Anyone with Yankee roots is naturally predisposed to traditional-style houses. But in Southern California, for example, homes with classic New England features are hard to come by. And a lot of people who transplant from one coast to the other crave the architectural details lacking in the modern or casual–style houses that prevail in certain parts of the country.

Thankfully, whether you want to increase the character quotient in a home you're trying to sell or warm up one you want to keep, adding architectural details can be done to varying degrees and without necessarily breaking the bank. If you want to evoke a Cape Cod–style structure, for example, instead of going overboard and trying to create period-piece interiors with traditional styling, you might add refined details that create a sense of history. Simple beadboard paneling, along with chair rails, can create a traditional theme. Or crown moldings and baseboards can add touches of warmth and character.

If you plan to keep your home, you might want to splurge on custom millwork, but if you have a limited budget or if you plan to sell, you can buy lightweight, durable, cost-effective urethane moldings and wainscoting from sources like Fypon, Style-Mark or Ez A Peel. Home Depot and Lowe's also offer affordable prepainted wood or wood composite wainscoting, and other millwork and molding that you can fairly easily install yourself.

Just as houses without millwork or molding can lack appeal, houses with dated details can turn off potential buyers, too. If you own or have purchased a home built in the late 1950s or early '60s, for example, with undistinguished fake wood or pine paneling on a porch or basement space, you can easily give it a fresh, contemporary look by painting it white or cream. White-painted beadboard panels along the walls will add texture while keeping the backdrop light. You can also use mirrored walls and glass paneled doors to open up sightlines in small spaces.

Cabinets and Counters

Since so many people are investing in kitchen and bath upgrades nowadays, the surfaces in these rooms mean a lot to potential buyers as well as owners. They're also extremely costly rooms to renovate. And since materials preferences and configuration of these rooms is highly personal, investing in products that a prospective buyer may want to remove makes little sense. So unless you plan to keep your home, bypass an expensive redo and give them a budget-savvy update instead.

AFFORDABLE FIX-UPS

If your cabinets and counters are in reasonably good shape but need sprucing, you can give them a quick lift by cleaning and polishing them. Or you can simply paint dated cabinets or freshen them very affordably with new hardware. Another budget-smart option is to replace the doors and drawer fronts on standard-size cabinets.

As with tile walls, kitchen and bath counters made of dingy tile or tile in a dated color can be quickly and efficiently refreshed with a professional resurfacing treatment. One national franchise to consider is Miracle Method. A small tile counter can be updated in less than a day for about $400 to $500.

An affordable way to update kitchen counters to a higher-quality material is to purchase a precut slab of granite or solid surfacing material, such as Silestone or CaesarStone, from home improvement stores like Lowe's or Home Depot. These are available only in standard sizes, however, so you can't customize them.

INVESTING IN THE FUTURE

You can also use these approaches to give budget-savvy upgrades to these surfaces in a home your plan to keep. If you're willing to invest for the long-term, however, then invest in higher-quality cabinets with custom storage options, which will make your life more

TOP: **A shelf above the door links to the cabinets and provides a display area.**

BOTTOM: **The marble-encased tub with matching counter surfaces looks out over a private garden and produces an elegant spa-like ambience.**

RIGHT: **Thick white CaesarStone counters introduce a clean contrast to the dark wood cabinets and provide a sleek, easy-care surface for a contemporary kitchen.**

comfortable and efficient. Cabinets made of compressed fiberboard or laminate can start to erode in areas around the sink or next to a dishwasher, where water is inclined to leak, and will eventually need to be replaced.

If you're keeping your home, employing decorative cabinet details and counter surface materials can add personality in baths, kitchens, bar areas and other entertainment rooms to complement your style. Remember that some stone surfaces, such as limestone, marble and soapstone, are porous and prone to stains, and need to be sealed regularly. So as with tiled wall surfaces, be sure to choose a counter surface that's practical as well as beautiful.

Antiqued limestone countertops complement the French country–inspired cabinets and enhance the old-world spirit of this Berkshires kitchen designed by Robyn Keller of Millbrook Custom Kitchens.

CEILINGS AND FLOORS

The quality of the ceilings and floors in your rooms can have a major impact on the real and perceived value of your home. If you want to sell your home, be sure these surfaces are as clean and visually appealing as possible. If you plan to keep your house and the floors and ceilings are less than desirable, think long-term. Any investment you make in durable, quality materials will reward you with comfort and satisfaction, often for as long as you live in your home.

Ceilings: Beauty and Function Overhead

The ceilings of a room are more important than you think. Designers sometimes refer to the ceiling as the fifth wall and see it as an opportunity for adding color or architectural character. In the 1970s contractors saved money on creating smooth or hand surface–textured ceilings and used a spray-on technique to apply what is commonly referred to as "popcorn ceilings." With smooth or surface-textured ceilings preferred today, rooms with popcorn ceilings are typically viewed as eyesores by homeowners and potential buyers alike. If you've got a room with one of these ceilings, you'll probably want to fix it, whether you plan to sell your home or live in it. For information on how to safely remove a ceiling like this yourself, visit *naturalhandyman. com/iip/infpai/popcornoff.html*. Better yet, call a professional. Since some of these ceilings contain asbestos, the job can be hazardous as well as difficult.

Designed by Mark Christofi, a beam and flatboard ceiling adds character to a remodeled contemporary California house.

If you have a ceiling that's been covered up with acoustic ceiling tiles, consider removing or covering up the tiles and finishing it with a flat surface, too. Doing so will make a home easier to sell and more appealing to live in. If you want to simply cover it up, there are products on the market similar to wallpaper that conceal a multitude of sins and eliminate the need to fill in the tile seams. Among these are Flexi-Wall Systems' Plaster In A Roll and Faster Plaster. Plaster In A Roll is a one-step, crack-proof wall covering that comes in three decorative textured weaves that absorb sound much like acoustic tiles do. Faster Plaster is a two-step upgrade to most finishes. After applying it, you can finish with paint. This product can also be used to cover cinder blocks, wallboard, paneling or tile.

You can also remove the tile and the furring strips attached to the lath and plaster ceiling, and install drywall directly against the ceiling. But because with old acoustical tile you need to be concerned about the presence of asbestos, you should wet a small area of the tile, cut a 1-inch-by-1-inch sample using a utility knife

(power tools will send asbestos fibers airborne) and send it to an independent laboratory in a ziptop plastic bag for analysis (look for "Asbestos Consulting & Testing" in the yellow pages). If the sample tests positive and you want to have the tile removed, enlist a contractor specializing in the removal of asbestos. They can be found in the yellow pages under "Asbestos Abatement." Or contact your local air pollution control authority. They can provide information about asbestos abatement for homeowners who want to and are able to do the work themselves.

If you opt to install drywall directly to the ceiling tiles, fasten it directly into the furring strips under the tiles. Locate these furring strips with a stud finder. You'll need a building permit, though, if you decide to hang drywall. A permit is not necessary if you apply either of the two Flexi-Wall products.

If you plan to keep your home and want to add interest or character to a plain ceiling, consider adding beams or crown moldings. A coffered ceiling grid is another appealing option to lend substance and a sense of intimacy to a room with no bones.

Along with granite counters and white-painted cabinets, a coffered ceiling in the kitchen of a new California home designed by Stewart Allen gives the room the look and feel of an older home.

Floors: Substance Underfoot

The right flooring is essential to support the function and character of your home. Given the high cost of many flooring materials as well as installation, your best bet if you want to sell your home is to mop, polish, vacuum or steam-clean the floors you have to get them into the best shape possible for viewing by potential buyers. The same holds true for a home you want to keep. You can also use a rug, which you can take with you when you move, to cover less-than-perfect floors and help define seating areas.

If you plan to sell or live in a home with damaged floors, consider refinishing or repairing them first. If you must replace them, do your homework before you take the plunge on any new flooring.

CHOOSING A MATERIAL

With so many options to choose from—cement, hardwood, laminate, tile, stone, carpet, cork and linoleum—the most important decision is to select a floor surface that's appropriate for the spirit and use of the room. For example, invest in durable flooring and finishes, such as hardwood, stone or laminate, for high-traffic areas, and reserve costly wool or silk carpets for little-used spaces, such as bedrooms. The region in which your home is located will also influence your choices. Wood floors add warmth to houses in cooler climates, but stone and tile work better in humid or hot areas.

Carpet

It should come as no surprise that carpeting is the top floor-covering choice in the United States. It is soft underfoot, forgiving of less-than-perfect subfloors, comes in thousands of colors, weaves and textures, dampens sounds and can be budget-friendly. The single most important thing in choosing it is to understand your lifestyle and select carpet that will stand up in places where it will get the most wear. The trick is to avoid abrupt transitions between areas. It's more pleasing to stay with a basic tone and coordinate choices for continuity in texture and pattern.

CARPET FIBERS

More than 90 percent of the carpeting on the market is made of synthetic fibers. Since fibers have different qualities, be sure to match the material to the wear you'll give your carpeting.

Nylon Found in almost 75 percent of carpets, nylon is valued for its ability to spring back. Even with wear, it returns to how it's supposed to look. It also holds color well, resists stains and is easy to clean.

Frieze and shag carpets like this have tightly twisted fibers that curl in different directions to help hide footprints and vacuum tracks.

Polypropylene Because it is not very resilient, this fiber most often is used in looped pile carpet, such as berbers. It is naturally stain- and fade-resistant, though it has a tendency to attract oily soils. The second leading fiber choice, it comes in a limited color range.

Polyester Though not as resilient as nylon, polyester carpet is known for its softness, color clarity and its stain- and fade-resistance. It is an economical choice that is used most often in thick-cut pile and textured styles.

Natural fibers Of the non-synthetic choices—wool, sisal, jute, sea grass, silk and cotton—wool is probably the best overall performer, offering rich color and durability. It also cleans well. However, it is the most expensive fiber.

PADDING

Also called the "cushion," proper padding makes carpeting more comfortable underfoot, provides insulation and noise reduction, and prolongs carpet life. Don't go cheap just because it's hidden. Think of it as insurance that will protect your investment.

All types of padding come in various densities and thicknesses, from ¼ inch to 7/16 inch. Reserve thick padding for low-traffic areas, since padding that gives easily will let carpet "overflex" or bend easily, shortening its life and putting stress on the seams. Generally, high-traffic areas require thinner, denser padding. Check the manufacturer's padding recommendation for a specific carpet. If padding is included in the carpet price, consider upgrading to get exactly what you need.

Fiber May be jute, cotton, wool, horsehair, felt or synthetic; works well beneath berber carpets, good in heavy-traffic areas.

Slab rubber Good for high-traffic areas, it resists crushing and indentation from furniture.

Foam May be rebond or high-density polyurethane. Both provide good insulation and can be cushy in a bedroom.

Frothed foam Made of super-dense urethane, it is a very low-VOC (volatile organic compound) option that can be used under all carpet types, is long-lasting and reduces furniture indentations.

FIVE BASIC STYLES OF CARPET

Saxony or plush The most luxurious choice, each yarn of this type of carpet has a uniform height and finish, offering a smooth look and soft feel for formal or little-used rooms. Plush carpet is prone to showing footprints or vacuum tracks.

Looped The yarn tips of this carpet are looped, not cut, providing a rounded surface that is extremely durable. Berbers are the best example of looped carpet, which often is used in casual family rooms, dens and some high-traffic areas. It comes in solid colors, flecks and patterns.

Frieze Frieze (pronounced *free-ZAY*) carpets have a cut pile and are workhorses that perform well anywhere, even in high-traffic areas. Each strand of yarn is twisted tightly and easily bounces back into place. The surface looks textured and hides footprints and vacuum tracks well.

Textured This type of carpet has alternating twists of yarn, creating a two-tone appearance. It provides a more casual look and wears well.

Cut-and-Looped The patterns of this carpet style are created through the combination of some cut yarns and some looped yarns. With its carved appearance, it can be found in both casual and more formal settings. This type of carpet stands up well in high-traffic areas and the texture helps hide stains.

PRICE CHECK

Carpet cost generally is less than any other floor covering, but comparisons can be tricky because wood and ceramic flooring are usually quoted per square foot, not per square yard. Divide the square-yard cost by 9 to determine the square-foot price. Always confirm whether the price covers padding and installation.

GOOD Up to $20 per square yard You'll find polyester and polypropylene in cut-and-loop pile styles. Solid colors will dominate, with flecked looks and simple patterns at the upper end of the range.

BETTER $20 to $30 per square yard In addition to better polyesters, nylon, with its proven wearability, and berber styles appear in this range. Look for more color and pattern choices here as well.

BEST $40 per square yard and up More complex nylon weaves and patterns, as well as natural fibers such as wool and silk.

PROLONG CARPET LIFE

- Use doormats outside your home's entrances and runners inside to help reduce soil and moisture in high-traffic areas. Clean or replace them regularly.

- Vacuum often. Tiny particles of dirt abrade and wear down the carpet pile. Vacuum at least twice a week using an upright vacuum with a beater bar.

- Keep dark colors from fading by closing draperies or blinds when sunlight beats down on the floor. Consider low-E glass or adding film to windows to reduce the harm caused by the sun's rays.

- For food and beverage stains, immediately pick up what remains of the spill and then blot (don't rub) the area. Rubbing or scrubbing will push the stain into the carpet. Use a cloth dipped into warm water with a small amount of mild detergent.

- Keep all strong chemicals and bleaches away from your carpet.

- Professional cleaning using hot-water extraction can be done every 12 to 18 months to refresh the look of your carpet.

INSTALLATION

Installation is best left to the pros. To ensure a precise quote, shop with a floor plan and the dimensions of your room in hand. Your salesperson should also visit your home and take exact measurements, checking subfloors, trims and site specifics. Along with the cost of the carpeting and padding, your quote should include a per-yard installation charge and fees for removing trim. Before installers arrive, you'll need to clear the rooms or arrange ahead of time to pay the installers to do it. Be sure you understand the terms of the warranty; with normal wear and care, most carpeting is guaranteed for up to 20 years. For more information on carpets, visit the websites of the Carpet and Rug Institute, *carpet-rug.org*, and the World Floor Covering Association, *wfca.org*.

RIGHT: The pattern in the flatweave rug in the dining room of this coastal home designed by Jackie Higgins recalls the pattern of a boardwalk and suits the relaxed setting.

OPPOSITE, TOP: A laminate floor looks like wood, but is actually a durable, more affordable alternative to the real thing.

Laminate Floors

Today's wood- and stone-look laminates have come a long way from the bland, fake-looking selection of oaks in various shades of medium brown and one-dimensional-looking faux stones. Flooring manufacturers are keeping pace with the trend toward exotic woods and unique finishes, offering realistically distressed surfaces, beveled edges, unusual wood grains, and colors that range from near-white to deep chocolate-brown.

What's new Look for rustic textures, whitewashed pine and subtly tinted surfaces. Also gaining popularity are faux versions of expensive and exotic African, Asian and South American woods, such as teak and merbau. Closer to home, butternut, hickory and wild beech floors offer classic American style. Registered embossing, matte grout lines and glossier finish on tiles create more realistic versions of slate, limestone, marble and brick. The good news about this trend: Consumers can have floors with the look of rare exotic woods or costly stone without depleting either our natural resources or their pocketbooks.

Installation Quick-install laminates allow you to easily upgrade your floors yourself. Planks are constructed with tongue-and-groove edges on all four sides so they snap into place. For extra water resistance, some laminates have pre-glued edges or are designed to be installed with a specially formulated glue to lock the planks together.

Cost Laminate flooring's cost varies with style and quality. In general, figure a laminate floor will be approximately one-third to half the price of its natural-wood or stone counterpart. Direct-pressure laminates, labeled "DPL," are suitable for most residential uses and are less expensive than high-pressure laminates (labeled "HPL"). The cost of an underlayment to cover subfloors will vary depending on the surface that will be covered. A big cost-saver, however, is the do-it-yourself factor, since homeowners who might shy away from installing hardwood floors are often willing to tackle putting in laminate floors.

GLOSSARY

Click-in floors Also known as glueless laminate floors, they lock with tongue-and-groove construction instead of glue.

Tongue-and-groove These boards have a lip along one edge that locks into a neighboring indentation for installation.

Floating floors So called because they are not attached directly to the subfloor but "float" above it, floating floors easily expand or contract with the room's climate.

High-density fiberboard HDF, as it is known, is the inner-core, structural layer of laminate floors.

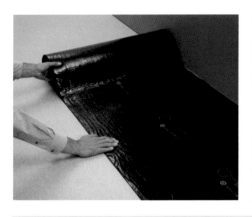  

EASY MAINTENANCE

- Vacuum with the brush attachment or damp-mop with plain water, a mild solution of water and vinegar, or water and liquid floor cleaner. Never use abrasive cleaners or steel wool to clean a laminate floor, and wipe up spills as soon as possible.

- Protect against scratches by lifting, not dragging, heavy furniture across the surface, or use pads to move items. Consider placing casters or felt pads beneath furniture legs, and avoid tracking in gritty dirt.

A word on subfloors In general, laminate floors can "float" above existing surfaces, without being attached to the old floor. Laminates can be installed directly over old tile, vinyl, wood or concrete but not over carpet. You must remove carpet and pads before installing laminate flooring. Unless the laminate flooring has an attached underlayment, most subfloors will require installing a polyurethane underlayment beneath the laminate planks. The composition of the underlayment will vary depending on whether it is needed to block moisture, as on a concrete basement floor, or to deaden sound.

TREND WATCH

Fabulous at faking it, laminates are showing up in a wider range of fashionable styles.

Stone Laminate brings the look of stone tiles without the hassle. It's also more resilient than real stone, so it's more forgiving to stand on. The tiles have the texture and appearance of glazed stone perfect for a kitchen or bath.

Dark Rich, dark wood tones are becoming a popular choice for floors, mimicking trends in cabinetry, and adding warmth to a casual decor.

Exotic Add the lush look of exotic woods without the luxurious price tag.

Ceramic and Porcelain Tile

Glazed ceramic tile is easy to care for and durable. It resists stains, odors, water, fire and dirt, and can be cleaned up with a damp mop or sponge and common household cleaners. Properly installed, ceramic tile will outperform and outlast nearly any other floor covering product created for the same application. It is also a natural product made of clay, other naturally occurring minerals, and water, so it is environmentally friendly. Glazed tiles have a coating, which is fired to give the tile a specific color and finish.

Not only is this flooring option practical, it also offers limitless design possibilities in color, style, shape and finish, giving you the opportunity to create a very personal design statement if you plan to keep your home. If you want to sell your home now or in the future and are willing to replace or install a tile floor, opt for understated tiles in white, cream or beige, which have more universal appeal and will help add value to your home.

If you need to replace a broken floor tile but didn't save spares from the initial installation, you have a few options. First, contact your tile layer or supplier and see if they have any leftover stock. If not, ask for the tile's make and model number. The Ceramic Tile Distributors Association (800-938-2832; ctdahome.org) can help you locate the manufacturer and order a replacement. Unfortunately, tiles are produced in limited runs, so you may not be able to find an exact duplicate. If that's the case, decorative tile manufacturers, such as Dunis Studios (830-438-2996; dunisstudios.com) and North Prairie Tileworks (612-871-3421; handmadetile.com), can create a new tile, color-matched to a sample of the original. This service starts at about $35 for each tile, peanuts compared to what it costs to replace an entire floor.

ABOVE: White tile floors accented with contrasting black insets add interest to an all-white bath.

OPPOSITE, BOTTOM: Real wood floors, whether they are veneers on an engineered substrate or solid wood, always add value to a home.

Wood and Stone Floors

Everyone loves beautiful natural wood or stone floors, both of which will increase the value of your home. Hardwood floors come in virtually any kind of wood imaginable, from classic North American species such as oak, cherry and walnut to exotic woods such as fruitwood, merbau and teak. Environmentally conscious options include flooring made from trees grown in sustainable forests; reclaimed flooring, which displays imperfections that add a unique patina; and bamboo, which is actually a grass, but is very durable. If you want to install new wood floors in a home you plan to keep, be sure to choose a wood that meshes with the style of your home or the style you aim to create.

Wood floors also come in a wide range of widths, stains and finishes. Planks can either be solid wood in various thicknesses or they can be engineered planks that feature a thinner layer of natural hardwood affixed to an engineered substrate, which can be applied directly over a concrete floor. Solid wood floors must be applied over a plywood subfloor. If you want to install new wood floors in your home, contact a professional to help you choose the best floor for your setting. Since wood floors can put a sizable dent in your wallet, get quotes and referrals from several installers before proceeding. The starting price for wood floors is about $3.50 per square foot, and installation and removal of existing floors can triple or quadruple the cost of flooring.

If you already have wood floors that need refinishing to make them appealing to a prospective buyer, you can rent a sander and try to refinish yourself. This is a daunting process, however, since sanders are difficult to control, generate heaps of wood dust and can damage your floors if not handled properly. You'll also need to apply a polyurethane or urethane finish, both of which are difficult to use and produce dizzying fumes. For a more expensive but less labor-intensive and risky option, contact a professional in your area to see whether refinishing is possible and get an estimate. Some floors can be refinished using what is known as a screening process, which some companies define as sandless refinishing. (Though some professionals point out that even the screening process produces some fine dust and is suitable only for certain surfaces.)

For a natural, nontoxic DIY refinishing option, consider using a soy-based gel finish remover and a tung oil finish. Although it's a messy, goopy process, there is no sanding involved. A tung oil finish needs to cure before you place a rug on it; this process can take up to a month. One source for these products is The Real Milk Paint Company (*realmilkpaint.com*).

Natural stone floors are typically more expensive than stone tile floors, but either variation will almost always increase your home's resale value. Stone floors range from granite, slate and marble to travertine and limestone. Although stone is difficult to cut and lay, modern tools have increased the speed and efficiency so that natural stone is now accessible to all and is beloved for its durability, personality and aesthetics.

Different stones have different levels of hardness and porosity, so as with any costly floor material, do your research before investing in a stone floor and choose a material that suits your purpose as well as style.

Vinyl, Linoleum and Cork

Thanks to huge advancements in styling and manufacturing technology, resilient or vinyl floors are more appealing than ever and can mimic the look of ceramic, stone, and even wood. In fact, few floor covering categories offer you the selection, styling, ease of maintenance and value of vinyl. So, whether you plan to sell or keep your home, consider this versatile, affordable option as one of the easiest ways to improve the look of a dingy floor. Vinyl floors come in two forms, sheet vinyl or tiles, which look a lot like ceramic tiles (except that vinyl is flexible). Other natural alternatives to vinyl include cork and linoleum.

Installing a vinyl floor, or a cork or linoleum one, is difficult, labor-intensive and requires full knowledge of substrates, or the layer of flooring material that lies beneath the resilient flooring. As a result, the experts at the World Floor Covering Association say that doing it yourself is definitely not recommended. As with most any flooring, they strongly recommend you call upon a reliable, seasoned professional to install your vinyl flooring and that you ask your retailer for suggestions. You can find answers to almost any imaginable question on every type of flooring on the World Floor Covering Association's website: *wfca.org*.

ABOVE: In the kitchen of this home in the Berkshires, cork flooring stands up to heavy traffic, while the Oriental runners don't show dirt.

OPPOSITE: Durable rough-hewn stone floors add character and practicality to a contemporary kitchen.

QUICK FIXES

MAKE A STATEMENT Instead of refinishing a scratched, scuffed old wood floor, mask its flaws with bold stripes of white paint, alternating with stripes of the natural wood.

SHOW OFF Cover a stove hood with beadboard and adorn it with molding and finials to provide the perfect perch to display cherished china or ceramic collectibles.

OLD-FASHIONED CHARM Swap in swirled or crackled glass in place of pressed fiberwood cabinet doors. The not-so-see-through glass will help keep your kitchen looking open and airy, and, at the same time, hide the contents on those days when things are less than tidy.

SIMPLE UPDATE Give cabinets and kitchen drawers a fresh look with a new coat of paint and new drawer pulls. Use one style on drawers and a contrasting style in the same metal on doors.

Furnishings and Accents

A pair of matching transitional sofas, upholstered in cotton and linen, anchor this living room, while a navy blue wing chair picks up the hues in the draperies flanking the windows. A wood coffee table with a rush top adds a shot of texture.

FORM AND FUNCTION

Nothing has more potential to make or break the spirit of a room than its furnishings. As important as the style of the furnishings is their arrangement. If you want to sell your home, your goal should be to create furniture arrangements that will easily enable a prospective buyer to envision living comfortably in a room. You can do this by orienting furniture to accentuate the room's positive qualities, such as large windows that open onto beautiful views, and minimize its drawbacks, such as compact proportions or a lack of light. If you want to keep your home, on the other hand, and you're still in the process of acquiring the right furnishings, you can use what you have to gradually furnish your home in a way that's both beautiful and comfortable without necessarily starting from scratch.

So how do you begin shaping the decor of a room? The best place to start is with a plan. What is the room's function? Who will use it? What will its style be? If you're planning to sell your home, imagine the answers to these questions for a potential buyer. Make a list of the room's functions in order of importance to you. Then be creative about the furniture you have. You might need to move a piece from one room, leaving it a bit spare, and place it in another to create a complete look, for example. If you're keeping your home and plan to buy new furnishings, bear in mind that one size does not necessarily fit all. Purchase furnishings for each room based on who will use it most.

The Big Picture

If you want to sell your home, take a look at each of your rooms from the primary point of entry and try to see them through the eyes of someone viewing the spaces for the first time. To create the most appealing impression, keep in mind the essential ideas that any artist would apply to creating a striking tableau: composition, focal point, color, balance, line and scale. A well-appointed room will contain furniture that complements the style of the architecture and is scaled for the size of the room. Upholstery fabrics should vary to add visual interest yet harmonize with the room's overall palette. The perceived weight and line of tables and wood or metal furnishings should set off and balance the upholstered pieces.

If, upon looking at your rooms with fresh eyes, you see an appealing picture, then leave it alone, or simply freshen it by adding a new throw pillow or two for color and comfort. If, on the other hand, your furnishings were placed throughout the room without a cohesive sense of relationship to one another, then think about rearranging them in groupings that are as functional as they are easy on the eye. Even if you have purchased your furnishings expediently over time without a clear stylistic sense, you can still make the most of what you have by positioning your furnishings to maximize the spatial and architectural qualities of the room. For example, you might place a sofa to face a fireplace or a window with a view, set a coffee table or an ottoman in front of it, and flank the table with a pair of armchairs for a well-balanced seating group. If the room is large,

Skirted chairs and sofa create an elegant yet cozy ambience and keep this room, designed by Kate Singer, from looking busy by hiding chair legs. The subdued palette enhances the serene air.

you might float this grouping in the middle of the room and place a table behind the sofa to lend definition to its back.

If the furnishings you have in one room are out of proportion with the size of the room, see if you can place them to better effect in another room. A blend of eclectic furnishings and accessories can actually give a new home a cozy, lived-in look. You can harmonize them with color. A palette of creams, grays and golds, for example, can link mismatched furnishings, while pops of color or prints can add interest.

Another recommendation often made by professional stagers is to edit your furnishings and personal things, such as photographs, curio boxes or bud vases. Take a look at the things you have accumulated and decide whether they truly add value—be it practical or sentimental— to your life. If not, then don't hesitate to part with them. A clean, well-edited room will be as inviting to you and your family as it will be to a prospective buyer.

Smart Shopping Tips

If you plan to keep your home and want to purchase new furniture without working with a designer, make sure you do your homework before you buy so that you can get the most bang for your buck. Locally owned stores can be the best sources for furniture. They may deliver your purchase for less, offer a better warranty or return policy, or even assemble a piece for you.

The glass-topped coffee table and light upholstery fabric on the chairs and sofa reflect light, while chocolate-toned curtains, cushions, carpet and wood accents provide balanced contrast.

Their prices often are 15 to 20 percent less than big lifestyle chains—and often the quality is a notch better.

Don't buy furniture just because a famous designer's name is attached to it. The name doesn't necessarily guarantee quality; many designers have a variety of product lines with different quality levels. Instead, look to designer furnishings as a source for ideas and inspiration. When you find a piece you want to buy, you can often save 10 to 15 percent just by inquiring. How do you ask? It's simple. Just say: "Would you be willing to give me a discount?" And always ask about the store's return policy. If you buy something, take it home and find it doesn't work, you might have to pay a restocking fee if you return it.

Most people know what they like or don't like when it comes to color and pattern. Go with your gut, and then do plenty of comparison shopping to find what has the most appeal at the right price for you. Also, honor your lifestyle. Upholstery fabrics, for example, have come a long way, especially when it comes to ease of care and resistance to stains. If yours is an active household with kids, consider some of the newer microfiber fabrics. They're soft and wear well.

In terms of upholstered furnishings it's also important to think about continuity of color. Especially if your home has an open plan, have a nice transition between spaces. Otherwise, the effect can be jarring. With wood and metal furnishings, avoid the temptation to buy sets. If you buy a dining room table, try surrounding it with vintage or antique chairs. Another option might be to place two upholstered chairs at the ends of the table and wood-framed ones on the sides.

When you start looking, shop the entire spectrum, high to low. If you train your eye to understand the difference between a $12,000 sofa and one for $1,000, you can zero in on details you like when you buy in your price range. Combine high-end purchases with budget buys by waiting for clearance sales in stores and showrooms, checking out floor samples and visiting big-box stores. Also, before you go shopping, draw your room to scale and take the drawing and a tape measure along, too.

Choosing and Buying Upholstered Furniture

The perfect piece of upholstered furniture can do so much to enhance a room—add color and texture, provide a focal point, and reflect your sense of style. Even a first-time buyer can notice some of the hallmarks of quality: straight seams, tight stitches, centered and matched patterns, snug-fitting cushions, tightly sewn fringe and buttons. But there's more to an upholstered piece than meets the eye.

Against a serene backdrop of gray-blue walls, rich red furnishings and fabrics pop. Limiting colors to two or three tones keeps the look harmonious.

ADDED COSTS

Wood trim A carved, exposed leg is more expensive than a straight or covered one.

Trim Details such as fringe, tassels, decorative nail heads or contrasting piping will cost more.

Skirts A standard kick pleat requires less fabric and workmanship. Formal box pleats and tiered corners are hand-sewn, not stapled, and require added fabric.

Arms Some styles, such as rounded arms with gathered seams, require more fabric and labor, adding to the expense.

DESIGNING FOR THE SENSES

- **Create a sense of harmony** Include one or two pairs of things, such as lamps or side tables. Place smaller accessories to offset the balance slightly to keep the room from becoming boring.

- **Choose a color palette to match a room's mood** Employ soothing, muted colors in a bedroom for relaxation, brighter colors in a living room to spark conversation.

- **Place mirrors to enhance light** Instead of adding more lamps, strategically place a mirror opposite a window or chandelier to brighten a room.

- **Fill rooms with a pleasant scent** Fragrance enhances the visual mood. If a design is cool, pair it with mint- or lime-scented candles. For a romantic retreat, use lavender oils or potpourri.

- **Use contrasting textures to create excitement** Try combining glossy surfaces with rough ones: rustic hardwood floors with a soft silk rug, stone floors with untreated wood walls, a hard, lacquered table with a plush sofa.

GOOD (top): $500 to $900
A wood frame, steel springs, polyester cushions, basic covers.

BETTER (center): $900 to $1,500
A kiln-dried hardwood frame, steel springs, foam cushions with fiberfill wrap, some choice of covers and trims.

BEST (bottom): $1,500 and up
Kiln-dried hardwood, eight-way hand-tied spring construction, down-filled cushions, any choice of covers and trims.

CONSTRUCTION

Top-quality frames are made from hardwoods such as oak, maple or alder that have been kiln-dried so that they won't crack or warp as they age or when the humidity changes. Wood is better than metal because it holds screws better, which improves solidity. The joints of the best furniture are double-doweled and glued. Corner blocks that are both glued and screwed into place provide increased stability. Frames held together with staples should be avoided. When you sit down, the frame should not wiggle or shift, and there should be no creaking or wobbling. When you reach between the cushions and the frame, you should feel plenty of padding instead of wood.

The number of springs and how they're reinforced—both in the seat and the back of the piece—help determine a piece's quality and cost. Eight-way hand-tied springs (in which each spring is connected to its neighbor) enhance comfort, support and durability, and are considered the highest quality. Sinuous S-shaped springs running front to back and affixed to the frame also are good.

SCALE AND PROPORTION

Whether your rooms are large or small, long and narrow or spacious and boxy, the size and scale of the furnishings you place in them will make all the difference in determining whether they'll be comfortable and pleasing to the eye. Designers have an arsenal of tricks they employ to make small rooms seem spacious and bring large ones down to size. Whether you want to sell your home or keep it, you can benefit by choosing and placing furnishings as a designer would to make any room, regardless of its size, as comfortable and functional as possible.

Small Rooms

If you have a small room that has the additional deficit of being a little white box with minimal character, then consider employing some of these rules of thumb to make the space feel larger.

Keep it cool Paint the room a soft, cool aqua blue, which is a color that appears to recede, expanding the space and making it feel more restful. Choose solid-colored upholstery, accented with shades of white and soft cream. The peaceful colors also unify and expand the space and let the eye gravitate toward outdoor views.

Bring in texture Go light on furnishings and colors, but heavy on texture, combining a variety of elements, like slubbed silk on a headboard and matelassé covers and shams on a bed.

Shed some light If a small space is dark, it's going to look even smaller. Having only an overhead light is a big no-no in any room. It's not functional and it makes a room feel cold. Instead, floor or table lamps make small spaces feel cozy. Large lamps add height and scale. In addition, mirrors and reflective surfaces bounce light around and make a room look and feel much larger.

Don't clutter Be sure to have a well-organized closet. In a small living room, use side tables to display a few special pieces, which can be changed out with the seasons.

Add punch with artwork Even in a small space, an empty wall will look cold. Posters are inexpensive, and there's such a variety. Or try a grid of smaller prints with a similar theme to create the effect of one large piece. Frame a series of botanicals from old books, or surround black-and-white blowups of family photos with simple frames and big mats.

Think tall Draw the eye up with sheer panels mounted high above the window frame near the ceiling. They'll soften edges without blocking light and lend a sense of height.

OPPOSITE: **A bench upholstered in a leafy green links the garden setting beyond the window to this elegant dining room designed by Kate Singer. A collection of 16th-century drawings sits atop an antique sideboard beyond the mahogany table, giving the room a sense of quiet formality.**

ABOVE: **Details help pull a room together. The square shape of the pub table and stools mimics the backsplash and floor tiles. There's also a connection between the furniture's finish and the appliances. To select a wall color, the owner matched the hue of the bottle in the vintage print mounted above the table.**

LIVING LARGE

Raise the bed A taller frame lets you stow storage baskets under the bed.

Show some legs Sofas and chairs without skirts create a sense of airiness.

Glass is good Clear glass lamps and vases let you see through the object and experience the space beyond.

Scale back Smaller-scale seating makes a small room feel bigger.

Coordinate accessories A consistent palette makes a small space feel serene and gives objects importance.

Look down Small rugs can look like postage stamps on the floor, and make a small space seem even smaller. Instead, opt for a Berber carpet that's bound around the edges and extends almost to the borders of the room.

Mix and match Furniture sets often have more items than you need and can overwhelm a room. It's more interesting to mix pieces and make the space your own.

Limit pattern In small spaces, big patterns create busyness. Big patterns can also overwhelm, but if there's one you absolutely love, use it in small accents.

Break up seating In small living rooms, make room for reading lamps and water glasses by replacing sectionals with smaller sofas and side tables.

ABOVE: A super-tall bookshelf keeps books and objects contained in the small bedroom of designers Ray Ehscheid and Saverio Mancina. A space-expanding mirror over the mantel also reflects light.

OPPOSITE: Curtains mounted just below the crown molding add to the sense of height in the designers' small living space. A dining table doubles as a desk.

Use clever storage elements Three-drawer chests use a little more floor space, but when used in lieu of a nightstand you gain a lot of storage with them and they make a space feel luxurious. For storing bed linens, try a double-duty linen-covered bench/chest at the foot of the bed. In living rooms, try ottomans that open up for storage.

Splurge on custom touches in a kitchen Add value to this important room, especially if it's small, by combining standard cabinets with compact appliances and a few expensive touches. You can spend a bit more for marble floor tiles if you only need 20. A cabinetmaker can add trim to standard cabinets to make them look custom.

RIGHT: Mirrors—the bigger the better—are a great way to expand a room visually.

Large Rooms

Many new homes have open plans and rooms with extra-large proportions and high ceilings, so it's important to maintain balance in the space below. Nothing makes a big room look disproportionately large like tiny furnishings and accessories. How do you make an oversize room feel comfortable and inviting? The key is to make the space work for how you'll live in it. Start by examining what functions you'll want the room to serve—for family gatherings, for alone time with a book, for occasional meals or work sessions—then select and arrange furnishings that are up to the tasks. Large rooms can handle variety, as long as elements complement one another and don't compete for attention. To bring a too-large room down to size, try these tips:

Divvy up the space Execute a smart floor plan. A fireplace, for example, doesn't demand that a sofa be placed in front of it. If you stage one cozy grouping by the hearth, it can leave the rest of the space feeling lonely and disjointed. Instead, let the fireplace define separate areas for living and dining.

Pick a palette Having one color scheme throughout will make the room more cohesive. Warm colors like yellow, red, orange and brown heat up supersized spaces. Warm upholstery along with sunny accessories can link living and dining areas in a big room and give the room continuity and cheer. Teamed with linen-white walls, warm hues pop.

Accessorize wisely For large walls with little detail or trim work, try a grouping of nicely framed art or a grand framed mirror. Keep accessories focused and in proportion to the room size. A lot of small things can become clutter rather than points of interest.

Think twice Nothing pulls a large space together like repetition. Stage similar eye-catching focal points for both sides of the room. Try framing 20 squares cut from inexpensive wallpaper and mount half on either side of a hearth. Plaster sculptures of the same style and visual weight can link walls at opposite sides of a room.

Raise the comfort level A combination of upholstered seating fosters relaxation and, at the same time, heightens interest in a living area. Team a come-hither loveseat and club chairs with slipper chairs. Anchor the arrangement with a coffee table to afford a convenient roost for magazines or drinks. In a dining area, opt for upholstered chairs—appropriate counterpoints to a chubby loveseat—to encourage lingering.

Knock on wood Select furnishings with similar wood tones. Tables and chairs will look like first cousins if they share the same dark or light stain. In the same vein, paint a medley of furnishings—tag-sale finds and pass-me-downs—white, and presto! Instant unity.

Cover up One style of flooring throughout will pull the picture together. In lieu of separate area rugs, opt for one large one. Economical sisal is a great choice for a room that must withstand a lot of traffic. Sisal's nubby surface will interject texture and richness, too.

Pairs of light, leggy antique side chairs provide balance to overscale skirted sofas in this large room. Dark-toned wood accent tables punctuate the pale space with pops of contrast.

Brighten up Rather than creating a hodgepodge, select matching lamps. Copycat the color and style of the shades in an additional floor lamp to aid reading or sewing. If ceilings allow, consider a dynamic chandelier to serve as a punctuation mark and provide overall illumination. An oversize element brings personality to a lofty space.

Shelve it Built-in shelves are another unifying element and a cure for clutter. Install duplicate sets for books and CDs. Allow shelves in a sitting area to double as a bar for entertaining; use other built-ins as a handy buffet during parties. A tidy collection of baskets or pretty fabric-covered boxes can house everything from cocktail napkins and extra glasses to linens and silverware for setting the table.

Freshen up Sticking to your color scheme, enliven furniture groups with opulent bouquets of home-grown flowers. Or, dress a table with a small topiary in a fetching cachepot and set out a bowl of seasonal fruit. Notes from the outdoors bring life to a room.

Create contrast Try painting walls with nature's soothing tones, such as ivory and celadon, keeping colors consistent in adjoining spaces. A few dark accents—such as a mahogany table or bluestone fireplace—will keep a pale palette grounded. Also consider the view: Colors outside can have an impact on interior colors.

ABOVE: A patterned rug adds energy to a large room and defines the seating group. Furnishings float away from the walls, making the room feel cozy. The large mirror complements the weighty fireplace surround.

OPPOSITE: A warm honeyed hue on the walls brings down the visual perception of a large room. A mix of patterned fabrics on the armchairs enlivens the setting and tall table lamps suit the scale of the room.

Blend casual and elegant Interiors should be approachable—not museum rooms. Comfy seating, a mix of high- and low-end furnishings, soft fabrics: all contribute to an inviting look. To blend different periods, look for continuity of form and shape, then add an occasional unexpected touch, like a Murano glass chandelier, to keep it interesting.

Vary textures and materials Variety, well chosen, fends off a "done" look. Try mixing geometric patterns with touches of shapes from nature, such as a metal table with a twig base and shell-shaped wall sconces. A sisal rug, a coffee table with leather-wrapped legs, and fabrics in linen, silk and wool combine to create a subtle mix of texture and pattern.

Keep it light and uncluttered Bleached floors, touches of glass and reflective surfaces add light and sparkle. Skirted side chairs avoid giving a large room a "leggy" look. On windows, Roman shades made of banana fiber admit subdued light and shadows when closed. Simple molding details on walls subtly break up wall expanses.

Make it flexible An 18th-century English drop-leaf table can serve as a desk when leaves are folded down; opened, it can accommodate diners for an intimate meal. Consider using antique campaign chairs that can fold for storage. Introduce lightweight side chairs and side tables that can move easily and adapt to the event of the moment.

QUICK FIX Turn a garden urn into a side table. Give it a coat of paint, then top it with a cut round of painted plywood or MDF. Freshen a chair with a cover made from a fabric remnant.

The rug inspired the palette for the rooms in this open-plan home. Different paint and fabric colors distinguish each space yet harmonize with those in adjoining rooms.

QUICK FIX To make this upholstered screen, top hollow-core doors with batting, wrap with fabric and staple in place. Cover staples with trim and hinge together.

ARRANGEMENT AND COMPOSITION

Mix & Match

Mastering an ideal mix of furnishings in a room is no easy task. And when the pieces are of different styles or eras, the challenge becomes even greater. But nothing is more dull than rooms filled with matched sets of furniture. So you'll always want to set off a pair of matching club chairs or sofas with at least a few unique pieces to add energy and interest to your spaces. One key to getting a group of different furnishings to work together in harmony is to choose a piece of furniture or two that will anchor the room. In a living room, for example, that might be a beautiful chair or a work of art—though many designers believe the art should always follow the furnishings. Be sure to select this piece carefully, and the rest of the elements can be easier to choose. To create appealing furniture arrangements in every room, consider these expert tips:

Living/Family Rooms

Since living rooms and family rooms are public spaces, these are among the first rooms family, guests and prospective buyers will see after coming through the door. As such, their furnishings should be as beautiful as they are practical, and arranged in ways that support the activities in the room and facilitate movement through to other rooms.

Think about the big picture Select furnishings that relate to one another through form, scale or some other vital quality. To harmonize a collection of disparate pieces, try mixing only two or three styles. Living with an eclectic style requires good editing skills.

Unify with color A pale color scheme, accented with subtle blues and yellows, for example, sets a sophisticated tone and allows the shapes of furnishings to stand out. Consider whitewashed wood occasional chairs and ivory contemporary roll-arm sofas to blend with creamy walls. In a casual room, you might opt for bolder color or pattern for upholstered pieces, establishing continuity with a red, white and blue palette on furnishings to let them stand out against a pale backdrop. Or try the reverse, by painting walls a brighter color—sunny yellow or cool blue—and choose neutral or white slipcovered furnishings, or furnishings upholstered with textured fabrics.

Create contrast When your backdrop is neutral, it's easier to compose a room with striking accents. For example, black and espresso-toned furnishings, such as a demilune table and black lampshade, pop out in a scene and break up the uniformity of the palette.

Balance shapes A large modern picture frame with sharp angles can starkly set off a delicate Louis XVI–inspired armchair, creating a dramatic effect. But too many different shapes can be disorienting. To create balance, repeat shapes with pairs of furnishings. Also, be sure to balance the scale and proportions of furnishings. An extra-large roll-arm sofa will overwhelm a lightweight side chair by itself. Instead, flank the sofa with upholstered armchairs with similar weights, then introduce a pair of the lighter-weight side chairs as accents opposite the sofa.

Let things flow Bear in mind how one space relates to adjacent spaces and think about how people will move through a room and into another. Don't crowd furnishings, and make room for natural circulation paths. Allow 3 to 3½ feet of clearance around arrangements for movement.

RIGHT: Built-in storage next to the fireplace houses the TV. Nautical-look upholstery fabric on couches picks up the color of the navy-blue Roman shades.

BELOW: Comfortable furniture mixes with nautical accents in the living room. Ticking upholstery brings the formality of the chairs down a notch.

CASE STUDY 1

PROBLEM This couple has a small living room and when they opened up one end to add on a new dining room, they were left with even less wall space.

SOLUTION To make this space-challenged living room more family-friendly, designer David-Michael recommends some basic edits, storage solutions and easy furniture shifts.

The first step is to edit carefully. He recommends moving out the corner curio cabinet. The toys and knickknacks add to the visual clutter, and some should be relocated as well. Here are a few of his additional suggestions:

Paint A good paint job can breathe new life into a room. Try something warm with just a bit of soft color, like Ruskin Room Green from Sherwin-Williams' Historic collection. It's timeless, but not oversaturated.

Make the most of the TV area Leave the furniture arrangement as is, but get a flat screen. Either buy a wall-mount flat-screen TV, which would free up quite a bit of wall and floor space, or buy a more streamlined TV cabinet that is designed to hold a flat-screen television and double as additional storage.

Give the sofa a facelift If possible, invest in a new sofa, ideally one with flat arms versus rounded arms to maximize the space around the sofa and the cushions. Or get a slipcover for the existing sofa—something in a soft paisley with some rich golds, camels and maroons that are kid-friendly and won't show dirt.

Use pieces that do double-duty Instead of a traditional coffee table, use a large trunk. Durable ottoman storage cubes would allow the couple to get rid of the mismatched storage pieces they have now and create a more coordinated look.

Anchor the space To ground the space and make the room feel like one cohesive unit—especially since it opens to the new dining room—get a nice area rug. The rug needs to be sizable—at least 8½ x 11 feet. A simple floral design won't overpower the space, but will add some color, texture and visual interest.

Incorporate good lighting Add a floor lamp next to one of the chairs, and a wall-mount, swing-arm lamp next to the other (to preserve space).

PROPOSED LAYOUT Move out the curio cabinet and replace the bulky television console to make room for a couple of cozy chairs on either side of the TV, and introduce practical light fixtures.

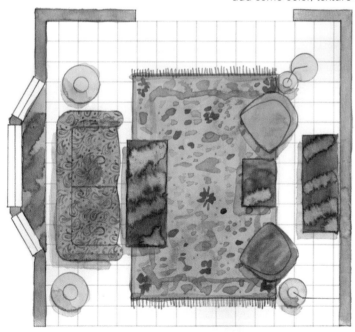

CASE STUDY 2

PROBLEM The owners of this bland living room have two kids and want it to be a crisp, clean space where both adults and kids can be comfortable. The large space has a great vaulted ceiling, but it feels cavernous, and the off-center placement of the three large windows is a challenge.

SOLUTION "The room needs to be rebalanced and warmed up," says designer Anjum Razvi. Some creative design tricks and accessorizing will help take the focus off the windows. Here's what she suggests:

DOS AND DON'TS

Do include plenty of storage. Family rooms accommodate many activities, including games that need a place to hide when not in use.

Don't forget who uses the room. In a house full of youngsters, easy-care fabrics and sturdy furniture are musts.

Do make things multiuse. Double-duty items eliminate the need for space-hogging furniture.

Don't clutter. Too many accents make a room feel busy and invite mishaps.

Do give things a lift. Furniture with exposed legs reveals more floor space, making a room look and feel larger.

Don't take it too seriously. Some playful design elements—such as movie posters—will set a fun mood.

Ground the room with a rug Try a subtle floral or geometric pattern with reds, greens and golds to add color and personality.

Paint the ceiling The walls are painted a golden yellow, which provides a nice starting point for the palette. Painting the ceiling, which is currently white, a lighter shade of the hue will make the room feel cozier.

Add a screen There's so much wall space that the corner behind the sectional is getting completely lost, making the off-center windows stand out even more. Adding a see-through wicker or metal folding screen here will bring some texture and dimension to the corner and help balance out the windows.

Hang a large piece of art next to the windows It will create a dramatic focal point.

Install window treatments To soften the windows, consider stationary panels in a shade similar to the wall color—perhaps a fabric with an open weave to add some texture.

Swap out the coffee table Choose a round table that can snuggle into the sectional. Since the sectional is very big and heavy, the coffee table should be lighter with clean-lined legs.

Add more lamps A perfect place for a lamp is on the console table between the sectional and the stair railing—perhaps something with a red ceramic base to add some more color.

Simplify the entertainment center A big piece like this is good to anchor the room, but there's too much clutter in it. Instead, group family photos on one shelf, and add large accessories—such as bright vases—one per shelf.

PROPOSED LAYOUT Taking the focus away from the off-center windows will help the space feel more balanced. A cohesive color scheme built around a new rug, and carefully chosen accessories, will give the room a pulled-together yet comfortable look.

A painted sideboard provides much-needed storage without consuming too much space in a small dining room. A mix of chairs around the table keeps the look lively, while a striped rug ties the colors of the painted pieces together.

OPPOSITE, TOP: A freshly painted vintage drop-leaf table and chairs add charm and function near a window in a small kitchen.

OPPOSITE, BOTTOM: Sleek barstools around a kitchen island allow family and friends to keep the cook company. Mid-20th-century chairs around the breakfast table are consistent with the modern space.

Dining Spaces/Eating Nooks/Kitchens

As primary gathering spaces for family and friends, dining rooms, breakfast nooks and kitchens tend to be the more intimate public rooms, where, in addition to a good meal, people share stories, ideas and laughter. So instead of treating your dining area as just a spot for meals, make it a friendly environment for other activities like reading the newspaper, doing homework or playing games—particularly if you don't have a lot of space in other rooms. Here, some expert tips on making these spaces inviting and comfortable.

Mind the traffic Furnishings don't necessarily have to take center stage. In a dining space that opens onto an adjoining living room, slide the table to one side and anchor the setting with a built-in banquette. It's more intimate and frees the path to other rooms.

Mix it up Rather than a clutch of matching chairs, opt for a nontraditional blend of seating to add interest, such as placing upholstered armchairs at the head and foot of a table and surrounding the rest of the table with Windsor or ladderback chairs. At the same time, pay attention to how many legs you're showing off. Too many and you end up with a jumbled look. As a remedy, skirt some chairs and consider a pedestal-style table. Or invite company to join the cook by surrounding one side of a kitchen island with sleek upholstered barstools.

Cast a glow A chandelier is wonderful, but isn't a must. Instead, consider swing-arm lamps, which can be practical and conserve limited floor space. Include dimmers and you will be able to adjust the mood according to whim. Add style and substance to a kitchen with a row of pretty pendant fixtures over an island or countertop.

Attract attention Mount a display of prints in matching frames as a focal point on a wall in a dining room, or place a collection of pretty plates in a wall-mounted plate rack in a kitchen.

Polish it off Edit accessories to fit the occasion in a dining room. Bring in a pretty cloth for formal nighttime dining. Then, the next day, bring in a tray of books, a cup filled with pencils and maybe a magnifying glass to achieve a library-like demeanor.

Soften up Soft pillows that complement your color scheme are great in a breakfast nook. Fashion a cozy niche for paying bills and writing grocery lists by placing a cushioned chair near the counter in a corner of the kitchen or at either end of a dining table.

Bedrooms

Bedrooms are sanctuaries—comfort zones for resting and rejuvenating at the end of a long day. Because they are private spaces, they're ideal rooms for self-expression and very personal touches. If you're staging a bedroom to sell, however, your best bet is to define the space with universal appeal. Clutter-free bedrooms are soothing, and bedding in neutral or pale hues will add to a serene effect. Whether you plan to keep your home or sell it, consider these tips for creating a beautiful, inviting bedroom.

Keep it soft The bed is the focal point of any bedroom, so give it the attention it deserves by layering it with bedding in different patterns or textures to lend interest. Fold a handmade quilt at the foot of the bed atop a vintage bedspread and toss a decorative neck roll in front of the pillows. Or fold back printed sheets to let a touch of pattern peek through beneath a plain comforter. For a romantic look, surround the legs of a bed with a dust ruffle. If you have hardwood floors, place a large carpet under the bed to keep it soft underfoot first thing in the morning and last thing at night.

Mind the bed Never select a bed without a headboard. It makes a room seem sloppy. In a small room, the vertical posts on a poster-style bed can visually raise a ceiling. And by not adding a skirt you can de-emphasize the bed and give a tight room an airier feeling.

Light it right Place table lamps on nightstands on both sides of the bed, and set the lamps on dimmers. Avoid an overhead fixture in the bedroom and use floor lamps to brighten corners instead.

Create comfort zones Designate a space away from the bed and ideally near a window for a vanity or writing desk. A comfy upholstered or slipcovered armchair provides a perfect perch for relaxing or reading. Team the chair with a small side table so you have a convenient rest for a cup of tea and books. A mirror or glass tabletop affords an extra bit of dazzle. Or create a cushioned window seat, with storage for blankets in drawers below. Pull up a butler's table to turn it into a cozy breakfast spot on Sunday mornings.

Keep it serene Cover windows with curtains or shades or both to keep out light and maintain privacy. If you have a television in the room, stow it in an armoire or built-in cabinet so that it's out of sight when you sleep—or show the room to a potential buyer.

Create focal points In lieu of a hodgepodge of things, hang a cohesive group of prints or pictures, using similar mats and frames, in a line above the bed. Extend the line past the bed if the room is small to make the wall appear longer.

Wrapped in soothing blue hues, this bedroom is the picture of serenity. A white armoire, vanity and night tables control clutter and keep the palette clean.

KEEP CLUTTER AWAY

Savor symmetry Use two of the same lamps, similar pieces of art and the same side tables to create visual harmony. A small room, especially, should be visually balanced.

Use space efficiently If you can't build out, build up. Use inexpensive shelves to house storage baskets.

Prioritize placement Never rummage through stuff you don't use much to access things you use every day. Put the daily items within arm's length—in easy-to-reach baskets or a storage bench at the foot of the bed.

Dream in color A soothing palette doesn't have to be dull. Spring green and charcoal, for instance, is a serene but not ho-hum partnership. Finishing touch? Wind a dark wallpaper border around the perimeter of a pale room, just below the ceiling. The eye-catching border will help define the space like a frame on a picture.

Pamper the senses Lovely linens boost the comfort factor. Personalize with monogrammed shams. For a visual treat, super-size one monogram and include a bolster or two. Incorporating favorite mementos like an embroidered pillow that depicts a family pet or an antique dish also makes a private retreat cozier.

Get organized To maximize storage, include a nightstand with both a drawer and a bottom shelf. Pretty fabric-covered boxes or lidded baskets are convenient for keeping necessities like writing paper and eyeglasses close at hand but hidden.

Customize If you want to write or eat breakfast in a bedroom but there's no room for a desk or table, commission a carpenter to make a bed frame with a rolling footboard/table that can be pulled up when you want to write or eat in bed.

Float your furniture Round glass-topped night tables provide surface space without decreasing visual space. They're also easy to navigate around since there is no danger of bumping into a corner. If you top them with tablecloths, you can stow books, reading glasses and remote controls out of sight beneath them.

ABOVE: The bed in this guest room is an heirloom from the family of designer Laurie Smith. Acrylic works on paper over the bed complement the patterns of pillows piled on the bed. An oversize oval mirror serves as a quirky foil for a side table.

ABOVE, LEFT: A four-poster canopy bed gives a modern room classic appeal. A leather bench and upholstered armchair increase comfort.

Plenty of storage above and below this desk carved out of the corner of a guest room keeps the space looking neat when family and friends come to visit.

Multipurpose Spaces/ Home Offices

As dedicated office spaces become more prevalent in the home, more manufacturers are creating products and furnishings that make them more stylish. No matter what your style, you can easily find chairs, lamps, desks and storage items to create a work setting that both suits your look and enhances productivity, too. Whether your home office gets a room of its own or occupies a niche carved out of another space, such as a kitchen, dining room or guest bedroom, consider the following rules of thumb to outfit it in a way that's as comfortable as it is functional.

Show some respect Many people spend fortunes decorating a living room they may rarely use, but they neglect their home office, where they need to be inspired to do creative work. Instead of treating your home office like an afterthought, approach it in the same way you would a living room, paying as much attention to design as you do to utility.

Choose the right light Never install overhead downlights in a home office space. They create glare on a computer screen. As an alternative, you could install a pendant lamp that projects light up to bounce off the ceiling and provide a soft indirect light. Or you can get focused task illumination with a couple of great desk lamps.

Make yourself at home A home office doesn't have to feel like a cubicle. Add homey touches, such as fabric on the windows instead of blinds and an area rug to warm up the room and anchor the furniture. Instead of using metal file cabinets in a traditional or cottage home, opt for lateral file cabinets that look more like furniture.

Mind the details Attractive desk accessories used to be pricey, but now you can get great-looking stuff for a song. Skip over the smoked plastic file trays and go for the faux leather, or ones with natural fibers in basketweave patterns instead. And get your odds and ends out of sight by storing them in handsome boxes or labeled containers.

Bathrooms

In contemporary homes, the bathroom has shifted from a room of necessity to one of luxury as more and more people turn these spaces into private spa-like retreats. And some statistics show that bathroom makeovers will recoup about 78 percent of their costs.

Whether yours is a powder room or master bath, a tiny room or an expansive one, sprucing up its fabrics, surfaces, fixtures and fittings will make it more appealing to a prospective buyer in a home you plan to sell. It will also make it a more inviting space for family members or guests in a home you plan to keep. Consider these trends in features homeowners now seek in bathroom spaces:

A separate tub and larger shower area with a glass partition wall rather than a stall with a door or shower curtain.

Natural lighting, if possible.

Multiple body sprayers or rain showerheads in the shower.

Warm neutral colors in natural materials, like marble or stone.

Drawer or cabinet space to reduce clutter.

A separate stall or partition for the commode.

Instantly give the space a lift without spending a bundle by adding new cabinet hardware, sink faucets or fresh curtains. Use halogen bulbs in light fixtures for the most skin-tone-flattering light. Sew your own shower and window curtains for a fresh new custom look with pretty, low-cost fabrics. Stow toiletries and brushes in baskets or better yet out of sight behind cabinet doors. And scrub grout until it's squeaky clean. If you want to plan your own bath makeover, consider shopping at outlets, such as Direct Buy (*www.directbuy.com*), which has showrooms throughout the country and offers surfaces, fittings and fixtures at wholesale prices

ABOVE: A tub set into the upstairs bay window affords a serene spot for relaxing. Shades that lower from the top allow privacy. The traditional tub and mahogany furnishings evoke the feeling of a beachside inn.

LEFT: Sconces flanking an overscale mirror provide light at the right place for grooming. The frame around the mirror gives it a furniture-like quality.

QUICK FIXES

One of the easiest, most affordable and eco-friendly ways to give your home a lift is by repurposing old furnishings or updating flea-market finds. Older pieces often have more character than newer furnishings and can be brought into the present with little more than a fresh coat of paint or a yard of upholstery fabric. And usually these easy updates can be completed in less than an afternoon.

TRAY CHIC Merge a weathered quartet of staircase balusters with a rattan tray to create a charming old-fashioned breakfast table. A metal dowel and wide ribbons secured at the tops of the balusters work in tandem to stylishly support the tray like an elegantly crafted table base.

FOOT REST Create a charming footstool with little more than a can of paint and a yard of fabric. To revive a tired bench, coat the wooden base with crisp white paint and re-cover its tattered seat with a playful print.

TABLE TALK Let a little paint turn a neglected demilune table into a pretty showpiece. Start by painting the entire table white and then add a coat of robin's-egg blue to the top. With the second coat of paint still wet, comb in a crisscross linen pattern for a touch of texture.

TAKE A SEAT Transform a humdrum side chair into a charming Scandinavian-style seat with paint and a new seat cover. The padded seats on most chairs, including this one, simply pop out. Just use a staple gun to attach the new fabric to the bottom of the seat and slip it back into place.

Soft
Touches

Against a neutral backdrop, furnishings upholstered
in solid-colored fabrics create a clean look. Plump
pillows and simple curtains add shots of color and
pattern. Dark wood accents keep the look cohesive.

After you've set the tone in a room by repairing, painting or enhancing the walls, windows, ceilings and floors, and once you've introduced and arranged a collection of essential furnishings to enhance its style and function, you're ready to inject some personality with soft touches. Elements fashioned from decorative fabrics—graceful draperies, crisp window shades, plump cushions, inviting bed linens and colorful slipcovers—don't just add beauty to a room. They're also incredibly practical.

Think of soft furnishings as grace notes that balance the hard surfaces in a room. Beautiful curtains can provide privacy and control harsh sunlight; an elegant floor-length tablecloth can bring a sense of grandeur to a hall table while hiding boots or umbrellas stowed beneath it; a quilted coverlet can add appealing texture and comfort to a bed.

And—as seasons and styles change—soft furnishings can be among the easiest pieces to switch out to freshen up a room for yourself and your family, or to make it more appealing to a prospective buyer.

The upholstered pieces feature a subtle herringbone pattern and are set off by textured damask fabrics on the pillows and draperies. The slipcover over the ottoman can be removed to give the room a subtle seasonal change of scene.

DEFINING GOALS

Given the countless colors, patterns and textures of the decorative fabrics from which soft furnishings are made—as well as the myriad ways in which these fabrics can be shaped into beautiful forms—it helps to return to your stylistic frame of reference to guide your choices.

By now, you should be clear about your style preferences and the style of your home as well as your furnishings, and the choices you make for your soft furnishings should support the visual point of view you've begun to establish. If you're cultivating a traditional style, you might choose floor-length draperies topped with a pleated valance to frame a window, for example. If a country theme prevails, then you might opt for gingham cafe curtains.

The next step is to home in on your functional goals for the fabric elements as well as what you're willing to spend to achieve them. If you're planning to stay in your home, you might invest in custom window treatments, for example, but would never make that costly choice if you're trying to sell it. On the other hand, since bedding is portable and you can take it with you if you sell your home, you could easily brighten a room with new bed linens either way. You should also factor in the style, condition and placement of your furnishings, as these will also impact the decisions you make about soft furnishings.

The function of the room is also important. Living rooms or family rooms, for example, are gathering places and the soft touches in these rooms are essential to establishing a sense of comfort—whether you plan to keep your home or sell it. As public spaces, these rooms are also places for hosting extended family and friends, and, as such, should be dressed to accommodate guests, too. With this in mind, the fabrics you use in these spaces should be easy on the eye. If you plan to sell, fabrics in neutral or solid colors and limited patterns will enable a potential buyer to more easily envision the space imprinted with his or her own style. If you plan to keep your house, you can opt for stronger patterns and colors. Public spaces will endure a fair share of wear and tear, so whatever fabric you choose be sure that it's durable. A spray-on stain resistant, such as Scotchgard, can help minimize cleanup and protect upholstery.

A dining room, on the other hand, is where food and drinks are consumed, so fabrics that can resist stains or be easily laundered are ideal for these spaces. Also, fabrics with warm colors that stimulate the appetite and have subtle or minimal patterns let the eye focus on the food and place settings. Whether you plan to sell or keep your home, fabric can add a comforting quality to bathrooms, where hard surfaces abound. Gathered sink skirts can cover unattractive pipes or conceal toiletries in powder rooms. Decorative shower curtains can add color and pattern, as can basket liners or laundry bags.

Once you've considered your stylistic and functional goals, then you're ready to take a closer look at the soft furnishings options at your disposal and explore how they can help shape and improve the spirit of every room in your house.

A ruffled bedskirt, fluffy comforter, trim neck roll and silk draperies transform this garret bedroom into a serene sanctuary.

Traditional silk panels take a nontraditional turn with elegant tassels, layers of casual pin-dot woven sheers and a bamboo shade. Chunky wood rings and a faux bamboo pole top off the ensemble. Three totally different elements and textures melded together create a more eclectic look, which is visually stimulating for a study.

WINDOW TREATMENTS

Whether simple and casual or refined and formal, window treatments can play a profound role in enhancing or even defining the character of a room. They can frame a view, support a color scheme, and add a sense of softness and comfort. They also serve practical functions, such as controlling light, creating privacy and providing insulation. Even the most thoughtfully furnished rooms don't look quite finished without window treatments, and even dyed-in-the-wool minimalists are embracing the benefits that clean-lined fabric curtains and shades can bring to a room.

If you plan to stay in your home and can afford it, investing in custom-made curtains or shades will reward you with comfort and beauty for years to come—and can even help you protect your furnishings from fading in the sunlight as well as save you money on your heating and cooling bills. If you're staying put but need to conserve cash, you can still get the benefits of custom curtains or shades if you're willing and able to make them yourself. If you can't sew, there are affordable longer-term solutions, such as semi-custom window treatments available through catalog or online suppliers like Budget Blinds, Smith & Noble, Great Windows, Country Curtains or Calico Corners. Or you can opt for ready-made curtains that can be purchased at places like Pottery Barn, Restoration Hardware, IKEA or Bed Bath & Beyond. You can also embellish ready-mades with custom touches by adding trims or borders yourself.

If you plan to sell, you can also opt for ready-mades and slip them onto rods with clip-on rings that you can easily remove and take with you to your next home. Putting curtains or shades on the windows of a home you plan to sell will not only enrich the rooms with a sense of comfort and style that will appeal to prospective buyers, it can also help you mask a less-than-appealing view or make small windows appear grander. However, ready-made curtains and shades fall short of custom curtains in many respects. They are usually unlined and come in just a few colors or basic fabrics. They are also available only in limited sizes and their headings are often skimpy or poorly scaled or detailed.

The architectural qualities of a room needn't dictate the style of a window treatment, but they will affect your choices. You might opt for shades, for example, to highlight beautiful moldings or select flowing curtains to frame a set of pretty French doors. If you want to sell your home and you're trying to correct a flaw, such as a too-small window, you can mount curtains high above the frame of the window and well beyond their side edges. Shades mounted outside the window frame can also make small windows look grand and heighten the overall sense of space. Or you might layer a sheer shade under curtains to cover an unattractive view while letting in light.

Practical Matters

If you plan to stay in your home, taking into account lifestyle issues (such as wear and tear in a family room or fleeting tastes in a teen's room) and location issues (such as potential sun and moisture damage in a beach cottage) is also important in choosing an appropriate style, as are other practical concerns, such as light, temperature and sound control. When you consider that the cost of fabrics can range anywhere from a few dollars to a small fortune per yard, and fabrication, hardware and installation costs can further ratchet up the overall price tag, you can see how important it is to carefully assess your long- and short-term goals.

BELOW, LEFT: Designer Jackie Higgins of Beach Glass Interior Design interprets blue-and-white stripes with relaxed formality in a bayside bedroom, with flat-front dress panels topped by a self-valance trimmed in rope tassels. An adjustable sand-colored shade offers extra light control.

BELOW, RIGHT: Hobbled Roman shades in a bold black-and-white print bring structured softness to the glamorous bedroom of designer Erinn Valencich.

SCALE AND PROPORTION

Whatever window treatment style you may be considering, the size and shape of a window will impact the possibilities of and limits to your options. The area around the window—on both sides, above and below—will also influence your choices. While there are no hard-and-fast rules dictating the proper scale and proportions of a window treatment, there are generally accepted proportions that are most pleasing to the eye. If you want to top curtains with a valance or pelmet, for example, designers often follow "the rule of fifths" to determine vertical proportions of a window dressing. In other words, the depth of the valance should equal one-fifth the height of the overall window treatment from top to bottom. The rule of fifths can also be applied to the width of a treatment—the window should account for about three-fifths the overall width, and the curtain panels, when open, should account for about one-fifth each.

SELECTING FABRICS

When choosing a fabric for curtains or shades, decide in advance whether you want to make a statement with the curtains or whether you want them to serve as a quieter backdrop for other elements in the room. Since everyone's taste in window treatments is so personal, your best bet is to go for the most basic and neutral choice if you're trying to sell your home or plan to sell it in the future. If you do choose a patterned fabric, consider the scale of the pattern in relation to the scale of the windows and other patterned elements in the room.

Also, unless your curtains or shades are sheers or very casual and don't require lining, always line them with a fabric that is similar in weight and fiber content to the face fabric to enhance the drape. If you aim to control or completely block out light with your blinds, or if you want them to provide a layer of insulation, you'll need to line them with a suitable material that will achieve your ends. Lining your shade will also enable you to protect your face fabric from dust, deterioration and fading. Choose shades of white or cream for linings to give your windows a cohesive appearance from the street.

The style of your window treatments will influence your fabric choice. Along with color and print, consider texture, drapability and how the material will stand up to everyday use. Loose weaves can soften modern rooms, but may snag easily. Nubby fabrics add texture to modern and transitional settings; heavier fabrics, such as brocades and velvets, give a formal air. Synthetics and blends can be more durable, less expensive alternatives to fine silks and satins. Working through a designer or a franchise specializing in window treatments will open an even wider assortment of options. Before you invest, bring home a sample to try at the window, observing how it drapes and how it looks in different lights.

ABOVE: French doors get a modern update when framed with tan linen floor-length draperies accented by a band of red. Threading a narrow rod hung just below molding height through grommets at the top of the panels and aligning the bottom band with the chair rail creates consistent sight lines in the room.

LEFT: Breakfast nooks beg to be showered in sunlight, so sheers are an ideal option. To make the most of this sunny spot, the gathered sheers here frame just the lower portion of the windows. The translucent fabric provides a soft backdrop, allowing the colorful tablescape to take center stage.

Curtains

After years of sheers and the simplest of shades, an emphasis on more substantial window treatments is beginning to emerge. While clean lines prevail in the newest styles, details are back—as are layered fabrics, overscale patterns, and color. Restrained yet creative headings, trims and hardware offer extra oomph.

STYLE TIPS

If you're creating custom curtains in a home you plan to keep, you might choose more formal panels topped with crisp pinch pleats, X pleats or box pleats, or softer goblet pleats, butterfly pleats or fan pleats for traditional settings. For very soft, romantic headers, a variety of header tapes can be employed to create shirred or smocked designs. For a contemporary treatment, consider simple grommets that slip through the rod. If space is tight, panels with grommets require less room when they are open. Rings at the tops of panels can achieve a similar look as well as add several inches of length to ready-made panels. For more casual rooms, whether you plan to keep or sell your home, consider panels topped with tabs, ties or rings. These styles are also simple for beginning sewers to make themselves and are easy to remove for cleaning. Pocket-style headers always result in soft or romantic curtains.

Another important factor with curtains is their length. Ideally, they should break at the floor an inch or two for an elegant drape. But many people prefer curtains that stop just short of the floor for ease of cleaning. Short curtains should be hemmed at the windowsill.

CURTAIN RODS AND HARDWARE

Hardware is also a key ingredient in the overall look and function of curtains. Formal drapes topped by a cornice or valance can be mounted on a mechanical track with returns, which turn back into the wall. But curtains topped with pleats or rings require a decorative rod made of wood, cast iron or other metal, and finished to complement other surfaces in the room. For contemporary curtains, brushed nickel and stainless steel rods, or flat or stylized rods in cast iron or bronze, offer a sleek profile. Painted ceiling-mounted exposed architectural tracks are another option for simpler, more streamlined curtain styles.

When choosing a rod it's also important to consider how long it will need to be, how it will be mounted to the ceiling or wall, and how much weight it can bear. If your window

Luxurious ring-top panels with soft box pleats in a gunmetal silk add a bold finish to a neutral living space. A sheer, silvery floral-patterned balloon shade echoes the curves of pottery and wood accessories, softening the room and providing semi-privacy. For extra polish, the shade is embellished with a decorative gathered header and the faux-painted finialed pole is accented with washes of metallics.

PROS & CONS

When it comes to draperies, you can opt for ready-made, semi-custom or custom. The choice depends on your budget and the difficulty of the drapery project. Here's what you should consider:

Ready-made

- Ready to hang
- Budget friendly
- Offered in coordinated collections
- Limited selection of patterns, colors and sizes

Semi-custom

- Wide selection of fabrics and patterns
- Less expensive than custom
- Accommodates unusual sizes
- Limited to styles offered
- Requires careful measurement

Custom draperies

- Virtually limitless selection of fabrics and styles
- Measurements, ordering and installation by a pro
- Most expensive option

is very wide and you'll need more than one center bracket to support the weight of the curtains, you might opt for a decorative traverse rod with a concealed track mechanism, or a ceiling-mounted architectural track, which can support the weight of large curtains and enable them to open and close over a wide expanse without being blocked by a bracket. Choosing appropriate wall anchors for the surface of your wall or ceiling is also essential to a successful installation. Ask your hardware store for advice on the proper screws and wall anchors for your walls.

MEASURING BASICS

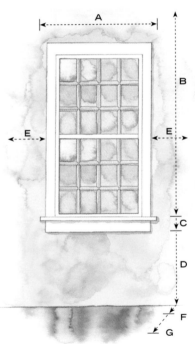

- Accurate measurements are crucial. Measure twice, just to be sure, and use a steel tape. Ideally, the horizontal measurement of your rod should be approximately 6 to 20 inches wider than the window frame, depending on wall space (A). For length, take one of three measurements from the top of the mounted rod (which ideally should be just below crown molding or halfway between crown molding and top of frame): to the top of the sill (B), to the bottom of the apron (C) or to the floor (D).
- The width of each panel should be 1½ to 2½ times that of the window. For sheer fabrics, the ratio is three to one. For lining and interlining, order the same amount of fabric.
- Allow for stackback, the amount of wall space needed to accommodate a fully opened drapery (E). It should be approximately one-sixth of the frame's width on each side.
- Most designers recommend a 1- to 2-inch break at the floor (F). If panels will be opened and closed daily, ¼ to ½ inch of clearance at the floor will let them operate smoothly.
- For a particularly elegant effect, stationary panels can be puddled, so extra fabric is gracefully arranged on the floor. Common allowances are 6 inches and 9 inches (G).

HEADS UP

A simple panel can become a showstopper topper with the right header. Here's a selection of some of our favorites.

gathered pleats
Topping curtains with a rod pocket enables them to be drawn into soft, gathered folds. Cut fabric 1½ to 2 times the width of the rod.

pencil pleats
Pleater tape creates a narrow row of folds that look like pencils laid in a row. Precise and formal, they hook to a rod or board-mount with tape.

French pleats
A classic French pleat is a triple-fold pinch pleat tacked at the bottom. Pleat spacing varies from 3½ to 5 inches, depending on fullness.

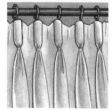

goblet pleats
Elegant goblet pleats leave the top of the pleat open to resemble a champagne flute. Pleats are lined to hold their shape.

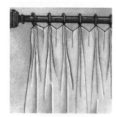

pinch pleats
Traditional pinch pleats bunch two small pleats together at regular intervals. Crisply tailored, they work well with interlined panels.

ruffle pleats
Adding a 1- to 2-inch header of fabric above a rod pocket forms a romantic ruffle when gathered on a rod.

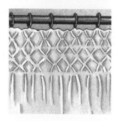

smocked pleats
Shirring tape creates a stylish hand-smocked effect along the header, falling with a skirtlike fullness below.

no pleats
Attaching clip rings or sewing rings to the top of a panel fashions a sleek contemporary header that stacks neatly when opened.

ABOVE: Unlined curtain panels with ruffled gathered headings bring a fresh feminine touch to a bedroom.

OPPOSITE: Flat Burberry-look taffeta panels are mounted on a narrow rod and flapped back tent-style to show off the unconventional red velvet lining. Rosettes on the British tan ribbon braiding on the leading edges of both sides echo the medallion holdbacks; a bamboo undershade controls light without blocking it completely.

For difficult-to-dress windows such as curved or bay windows, swivel sockets allow rods to conform to the window's shape. If there's no stackback room (see Measuring Basics) for the drapery to clear the window, consider a swing-arm rod, which will clear the window when open. Use knobs to hang stationary panels from loops; knobs also work well for draping valances around half-round windows.

Rods look best when hung high above and well beyond window edges. As a rule, if you can buy the hardware in a retail store, you can install it yourself by following package directions. It does take patience and accurate measuring skills, however, so it may be wise to call in an installer. Be sure the rod is sturdy enough to hold your fabric, and choose the correct screws and anchors for your wall, be it drywall, wood or brick. Most rods hold 1½ pounds of fabric per linear foot; check out heavy-duty rods for weighty fabrics.

Shades and Top Treatments

For those who prefer a simpler, more streamlined approach to dressing windows, shades or simple top treatments can add style and function. You might choose simple Roman shades or crisp roller blinds for modern spaces, ribbon-trimmed gingham shades for country settings or soft, richly gathered Austrian shades for a traditional or romantic room. If budget is a concern for you, opt for simpler shades, since gathered shades require more fabric. If you plan to sell a home and want a quick fix to dress up a window, some retailers, such as Ikea or Pottery Barn, also offer ready-made shades in standard sizes that may fit your windows.

Another option is dressing up windows with a top treatment. These may be used alone as a single decorative element or in tandem with drapes or blinds. Top treatments can either be soft, such as a swag or a valance on a rod, or structured, such as a shaped cornice. Cornices can be made of architectural molding, painted wood, metal or medium-density fiberboard covered with fabric. Some cornices are flat boxes finished with fretwork and topped by crown molding. Use simple, soft top treatments if you plan to move, and save the hard treatments for a home you plan to keep, since hard treatments are more difficult to install and would be virtually impossible to use on any other window.

MOUNTS AND HARDWARE

All shades and top treatments are supported by a rod, board, or structured and shaped foundation mounted on brackets. If you plan to mount your shade or top treatment on a rod and use it in combination with drapes, you might choose a double rod style, which will allow you to hang both from the same bracket.

Top treatments are always mounted outside and above the window frame, but shades, regardless of the type of shade you choose, will be either inside- or outside-mounted, depending on your goals. How you mount them will depend in part on the material and depth of your window frame. Your wall material and the space above and around the frame will also have an impact. Never opt for an inside-mount shade if your frames are made of metal or vinyl.

Shades, valances, pelmets and swags mounted to boards are attached to the wall with L-shaped brackets. When used in combination with drapery panels, whether operable or stationary, the board must be wide enough to clear the curtain, rod and brackets. Cornices are also mounted to the walls with L-shaped brackets and must also clear any projecting undertreatment. As with curtain rod brackets, always choose appropriate wall anchors and enough brackets to support the weight of any top treatment in your wall surface. If possible, try to affix at least one bracket to a stud for heavier top treatments.

OPPOSITE, TOP LEFT: A simple Roman shade in a tone-on-tone print adds a touch of softness and practicality to a kitchen window.

OPPOSITE, TOP RIGHT: Bordered with bands of checked fabric, Roman shades brighten a bedroom and tie into the color scheme.

OPPOSITE, BOTTOM: A pretty paisley London shade with inverted pleats in a contrasting check enriches the comfort of a writing desk near a window.

ABOVE: Simple solid curtain panels topped with a gathered valance provide a graceful frame for a cozy window seat.

RIGHT: Shaped valances adorned with beaded trim provide a character-filled dressing for tall windows and tie into the colors of the fabric chair skirts.

SLIPCOVERS, TABLECLOTHS, BEDDING AND MORE

Fabric coverings, such as slipcovers, bedspreads, tablecloths and sink skirts, are among the easiest and most cost-efficient ways to add color, softness and character to a room. Slipcovers can hide the flaws of a shabby piece of furniture, unify a set of mismatched furnishings or extend the upholstery life of new sofas and chairs by protecting them from the fading rays of the sun as well as dirt and grime. They also allow you to easily give your decor an occasional seasonal lift. Table and bed linens offer similar benefits. And covers made from fade- and stain-resistant synthetic fabrics can enhance outdoor settings, too.

Slipcovers

If you're planning to sell your home, you can simply freshen or unify the look of your furnishings with ready-made slipcovers. They come in a range of sizes and styles to cover different kinds of upholstered sofas and chairs. However, rarely do ready-made covers fit perfectly, so you'll typically need to fold and tuck the slipcovers for a crisper fit. You can also use T-shaped upholstery pins to temporarily secure the cover in place.

If you plan to keep your home, custom-made slipcovers will prolong the life of your furnishings and provide a tidier appearance. If your rooms are relaxed, however, ready-mades can still do the trick. For a semi-custom option, some furniture manufacturers offer affordable lines of furniture in a fairly broad range of fabrics for the permanent upholstery as well as fabrics in numerous patterns and colors for slipcovers that are specially made for the particular piece or pieces you choose.

If you're a seasoned sewer, you can also get affordable custom slipcovers by making them yourself. Use muslin, tissue paper or an existing slipcover to create your pattern.

CHOOSING FABRICS

The most common fabric for ready-made slipcovers is a durable, washable cotton duck, and this is a practical material for slipcovers you make yourself, too. Lighter-weight fabrics, such as ticking, gingham or cotton canvas, also work well for slipcovers. Unless you're creating a cover for a rarely used decorative chair, it's wise to avoid delicate fabrics, such as silks. Also stay away from heavy fabrics or those with a nap, like velvet, since the layered seams of slipcovers make these hard to work with on a sewing machine.

A folding screen covered with a neutral checked fabric serves as a stunning headboard. Against this backdrop, a small, exquisitely embroidered pillow stands out as the focal point.

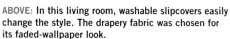
ABOVE: In this living room, washable slipcovers easily change the style. The drapery fabric was chosen for its faded-wallpaper look.

TOP, RIGHT: Contrasting piping gives an ordinary slipcover an eye-catching grace note.

RIGHT: An old dining room set gets an updated look with plaid toppers that harmonize with the curtains.

If you use slipcovers to unify several disparate pieces of seating in a room, consider making them all from the same fabric or choose fabrics that relate in color but vary in tonal value or texture. For a home you plan to keep, making slipcovers from different fabrics—a solid for a sofa, stripes for armchairs and a floral for a side chair, for example—will generate a more complex and interesting composition. If you choose this option, be sure to link the fabrics by choosing those with colors in the same palette. Including fabrics in a mix of large-, medium- and small-scale patterns will also keep the overall picture balanced. Remember that the style and scale of the pattern should relate not only to the style of the piece of furniture but also to its size and proportions.

Bench cushions and a table topper made of contrasting checked oilcloth brighten a kitchen nook with a fresh, easy-care cottage look.

Table Linens

Any kind of table—from side tables and consoles to dining tables and nightstands—can benefit from a tablecloth or fabric cover. Although ready-made dining table linens come in a wide range of colors and printed patterns, custom tablecloths are relatively easy to create and afford you the opportunity to link your table with curtains, chair cushions or slipcovers.

Dining table linens allow you to instantly change the mood of a room for different seasons or special occasions. Decorative table linens can allow you to hide an ugly or damaged table without replacing it. They can also allow you to hide clutter stowed beneath a table. Tablecloths can also dress up or dress down a table. Outdoor dining tables are ideal for taking chances with bold colors or patterns. They also lend themselves to creative tablecloths for different kinds of meals or styles of entertaining.

Since dining tablecloths for daily use are prone to spots and stains, choose cloths made of cotton or linen, as these fabrics are easiest to clean and can be machine-washed. But for decorative tablecloths, toppers or runners, go for decorator fabrics. You could also choose a poly-silk as a cheap, easy-to-care-for option to add polish. Decorative tablecloths are easy-to-change elements that can inject notes of color, pattern and personality into spaces to give them a low-cost lift.

Bedding

Fresh bed linens—such as duvet covers, bedspreads, coverlets, decorative shams and dust ruffles—can instantly give a bedroom a lift. And even if you plan to sell your home, they're worth the investment since you can easily take them with you.

Since bedrooms are very personal spaces, the bed linens, as well as the curtains and cushions in these spaces, should be soothing to those who sleep in them. But as with other spaces, if you plan to sell your home, creating as universally appealing an environment as possible is important. The trend in bedding is toward plusher, layered looks with decorative cushions and details, such as embroidery, piping and other trims. In a house you want to sell, you may want to avoid very personal looks, including offbeat or gender-specific colors, such as purple or pink. Fabrics for bedrooms should be soothing in color, limited in pattern and have a soft hand to create an environment that is serene and comforting. But in a home you plan to keep, the bedroom is the place you can freely indulge your tastes and shape into a personal haven.

If you don't have a headboard, you can easily use fabric suspended like a panel behind the head of the bed or even overhead as a canopy to create the effect of one. You can also freshen an upholstered headboard with a new fabric covering. Layering bedding, such as printed sheets, matelassé bedspreads and quilted coverlets, can also enhance the spirit of a bedroom and make it look inviting. You can get a decent set of bedding—often including pillowcases, shams, duvet covers and dust ruffles—in one package for a very reasonable price at price club stores, such as Sam's and Costco.

ABOVE: Layers of bedding with decorative accents transform a bed into an inviting comfort zone.

LEFT: A shaped headboard covered with a pretty toile gives a cozy room French-country appeal, while a flanged decorative pillow and pleated bedskirt complete the look.

PILLOWS AND CUSHIONS

There's no cheaper or easier way to give a room a lift than by introducing a few new decorative pillows. Simple throw pillows, cheery chair pads or decorative bolsters will not only humanize a room by adding a sense of comfort, they're also easy to switch out for a seasonal change of scene. And because they're small accents, you can afford to cover them with costly fabrics or embellish them with interesting trims that can add color or unexpected texture to a room.

Beautiful ready-made pillows are available at every price point. Because pillows are compact, you can also whip up a custom cover in no time. Since cushions come in contact with the skin, choose fabrics with qualities that appeal to the touch as well as to the eye.

TYPES OF CUSHIONS

Decorative cushions come in all shapes and sizes, and serve a variety of purposes in different rooms. Throw or toss cushions, for example, provide an extra touch of soft support to upholstered chairs and sofas. Accent pillows are often covered with highly decorative fabrics or embellished with trims, adding an extra dimension to beds and upholstered seating. Large-scale floor cushions introduce an extra layer of low-cost seating to casual spaces or kids' rooms. Cylindrically shaped bolsters and neck rolls can be used as arm props on daybeds or sofas, or as decorative head and neck rests on beds. Chair pads and boxed cushions add comfort to dining, outdoor or other hard chairs as well as window seats and benches.

DECORATOR TOUCHES

To add extra polish to pillows you make yourself, or to inject a ready-made pillow with a custom touch, consider embellishing a pillow cover with any number of interesting trims and decorations. Piping or welting provides a classic finish to the seams of all kinds of cushions, from a basic toss pillow to an extravagant neck roll. Other options for edging cushions include narrow flanges, wide ruffles, pleated borders, beads and brush fringe, among many others.

TOP: Piped striped cushions and pillows covered in a bold leaf pattern add casual comfort to a bedroom in a beach house.

BOTTOM: A slim line of decorative trim makes a tiny white rectangular pillow pop against a tufted upholstered chair.

SIMPLE FABRIC UPDATES

- Transform a lampshade with fabric. Use remnants and scraps. Spray on adhesive to adhere fabric to a shade base. Finish the edges with ribbon or trim.

- Cover heavy-duty cardboard boxes with fabric for coordinated storage. Wrap boxes as you would a package, using spray-on adhesive to affix the fabric to the cardboard. Cover the inside of the box with a fabric in a complementary solid or pattern.

- Make fabric bags with drawstrings to hide hair dryers, curling irons and other unsightly accessories in a bathroom. Hung on the back of a door, these necessities are unobtrusive but easily available.

- Slip fabric covers over a padded headboard. To create a headboard, purchase plywood (cut to size). Foam and batting can be purchased at a fabric store. Bind a sheet of 2-inch-thick foam to the plywood with spray adhesive and tightly staple batting over it for softness. Measure the material to fit over the base. Add 1 inch to width; double the height and add 6 inches. Measure two side strips 3 inches wide by the height of the board plus 3 inches. Fold cover in half crosswise with right sides facing, clipping cover allowance at corners around side inserts. Pin side inserts along each side with raw edges matching and right sides facing; sew with ½-inch seam allowances. Turn cover right side out, topstitch a 1-inch double hem around the bottom and slip over the headboard. Drill holes in its base and secure to the bed frame with nuts and bolts.

- Turn translucent or sheer fabric into luminous curtains that let in light while still providing privacy. Purchase inexpensive gauze, organdy, voile or netting. Measure two panels twice the inside width by the inside height of the window plus 6 inches. Hem sides and bottom with 1-inch double hems. Fold over the tops 1 inch, then press, then 2 inches more, and press again; topstitch to close, leaving ends of top hem open to hold the rod. Slide a tension rod through the pockets and install at the top of the window.

- Soften a corner, hide clutter or partition off a work area with a custom folding screen. Look for vintage screens at flea markets or estate sales. Replace worn or torn covering with a cotton canvas or printed fabric.

- Add color and pattern with a jaunty custom bulletin board. Stretch decorative fabric over a plain wood board covered with batting. Staple the fabric tautly to the frame. Crisscross and staple grosgrain ribbon across the surface, tacking it to the board with thumbtacks or nail heads at the interstices, and tuck invitations, favorite photos, clippings and cards under the ribbons to keep track of them.

- Mix and match to add depth and interest. Even if you don't have enough of one fabric to complete a project, be innovative. Upholster the face of a chair with one fabric and cover the back with another. Use a dramatic material for the back of slipcovers on dining room chairs and a more subtle choice for the fronts. Buying remnants can turn designer fabrics into affordable indulgences. Flea markets are another great source for unusual vintage fabrics. Use scraps of ticking to make charming place mats. Line the mats with felt or cotton batting for body.

TOP: A toile-themed guest room features wallpaper and modestly priced fabric that was made into bedding. A matelassé coverlet adds interest, as does the headboard's gingham fabric.

CENTER: On the window seat on a stair landing, a cushion's tiny checks pair nicely with solid pillows, which are covered with textured fabrics in complementary autumn hues.

BOTTOM: A half-inch-wide flange offers just a hint of extra detail to the vibrant tone-on-tone decorative pillow on this bed. The matelassé bedspread and satin coverlet add texture.

QUICK FIXES
Easy Fabric Projects

Fabrics provide an easy way to give rooms a fresh new custom look without the decorator prices. With very basic sewing skills, you can craft simple curtains and cushion covers with ease. If you don't sew, try brightening rooms with character-filled vintage textiles.

SHABBY CHIC Give a nostalgic flair to your next Sunday brunch with a casual picnic showcasing your flea-market favorites. A patchwork quilt makes for a colorful tablecloth on this antique dining set, adorned with a Ball jar vase, old-fashioned wicker picnic basket, and classic cake plate lined with vintage napkins.

BLENDING OLD AND NEW Many home-furnishing manufacturers offer vintage-inspired items that mix and match seamlessly with the genuine article. Here, antique candlesticks and dishes pair perfectly with newly purchased candles and cutlery designed to imitate traditional Bakelite. Completing the traditional tablescape are tag-sale napkins and a runner created from an old roll of linen.

SLIP-ONS Just a few quick stitches convert a pair of striped dishtowels into a pretty and practical coverup for a less-than-perfect dining chair. The towels' prefinished edges make them easy to work with for beginners.

TOWEL TREATMENT Repurpose a vintage dishtowel as a light-filtering curtain in a young girl's bathroom. Use clips from the hardware store to attach it to a tension rod or try doll clothespins for a fun touch.

QUILTED ACCENTS One advantage of older bed linens is that they are often softer and cozier than their modern-day counterparts. Antique quilts and blankets also work well as decorative accents, folded up at the end of a bed or displayed as a wall hanging.

Light

Windows in this second-floor kitchen could be left uncovered to let in plenty of natural light without the concern for privacy that would have affected a ground-level kitchen.

BALANCING NATURAL AND ARTIFICIAL LIGHT

You can brighten the rooms of your home by introducing the natural light of the sun through windows or skylights. You can also supplement this light with artificial illumination from table and floor lamps, chandeliers, sconces and other fixtures, including integrated lighting elements, such as recessed or cove fixtures. Your goal should be to provide sufficient levels of light to support the primary activities in any given room and, at the same time, to ensure that the quality of light is comfortable and glare-free.

While everyone covets a home with access to plenty of natural light, it's also possible to get too much of a good thing. Rooms with large, south-facing windows let in harmful light that fades furniture and fabrics and introduces excess heat in the summer months. East-facing windows allow in glaring light in the morning hours, while west-facing windows permit harsh light at sunset. And skylights can let in the scorching light of the noonday sun. Covering windows with shades, Venetian blinds, shutters or scrims can help control natural light, allowing you to maximize the best of it and avoid the worst of it.

Creating Appealing Lighting Compositions

Many of the principles that guide an artist—establishing a focal point, creating a harmonious composition, providing balance and introducing contrast—are as critical to a well-developed lighting scheme as they are to a furniture arrangement. Lighting designers generally think of interior light as falling into one of three categories: ambient, task and accent illumination. For the most effective lighting scheme, you need a combination of all three types—the pros call it "layering."

The first layer, ambient light, is an overall, evenly distributed, general illumination, and is often supplied by natural light or a diffused ceiling fixture or indirect cove light, but can also be provided by a mix of floor and table lamps. Task illumination is focused light directed on a specific area in a room to aid a person in performing a function. Task fixtures include pendants over a kitchen counter or a reading lamp near a chair or on a desk. Accent lighting draws attention to a particular area or adds sparkle and drama—think of picture lights or candlelight. If possible, aim to include a mix of these types of light in every room to create light compositions that are both interesting and practical.

Keep in mind that the fixture doesn't necessarily determine the quality of the light, rather it's the way in which the fixture is used. For example, sconces mounted on swing arms with shades that cast light downward provide task light for reading when placed beside a bed, but when mounted flush to the wall and topped with shades that direct light upward, they furnish accent light on either side of a mirror or over a console. Also remember that the finish and color of your wall surfaces, curtain and upholstery fabrics, and ceiling and floors will impact the quality of light in your rooms and vice versa. Sunny

This charming desk area is inundated with natural light during the day and artificial light from the twin desk lamps at night. Floor-length curtains control the sunlight when it gets too strong.

THE RIGHT LIGHT

Too much light makes a room feel garish; not enough makes it dull. Here are a few pitfalls to avoid.

Black hole An opening, such as a window or doorway to another room, that looks dark, especially at night, due to insufficient lighting on the other side.

Glare bomb A bright light that becomes an unappealing focus of attention. It is often created by a single source in the middle of the room.

Museum effect Too much accent light along the sides of a room. Like a glare bomb, it misplaces the focus and can cause eye fatigue.

Swiss cheese effect Holes in the ceiling created by an overabundance of recessed fixtures.

Layers of light ensure this room stays bright.

ABOVE: Natural light, a sconce, a chandelier and pendant fixture contribute to the well-thought-out lighting scheme in this room.

OPPOSITE: A pair of indigo blue pendant lamps glows over a sturdy reproduction table surrounded by old Windsor chairs in this comfy eating area in a kitchen designed by Jackie Higgins.

yellow walls, for example, will warm up the quality of light in a room. Shiny reflective surfaces will amplify and bounce light around a room, while dark colors, matte surfaces or textured fabrics, such as velvet, will absorb light.

Understanding the Quality, Level and Color of Light

Aside from the various layers of light, different fixtures and lightbulbs work together to produce distinct qualities of light. Indirect fixtures, for example, aim the light from a bulb upward to bounce off a ceiling, producing a soft, glare-free light. Direct fixtures project light downward, often with a focused beam.

There are two widely available types of lightbulbs for consumers: incandescent and fluorescent. The shapes of these bulbs influence the quality of light they produce—either direct and focused, soft and diffuse, or sparkling—and their wattage plays a role in the level or brightness of light they provide. In short, the higher their wattage, the brighter their light. Be sure to choose a wattage level appropriate for your fixture. Another characteristic of bulbs that influences the quality of their light is their color temperature, which is measured in degrees Kelvin. Light color ranges from warm to cool tones and is sometimes calibrated to mimic daylight.

Incandescent bulbs Bulbs in this family are known for their warmth and include traditional bulbs, known as A-lamps to lighting designers, and candle-flame–shaped bulbs, as well as the more energy-efficient halogen, xenon and krypton bulbs. The light from these bulbs can either be focused or diffuse.

Fluorescent bulbs Bulbs in this family include the long, narrow or circular tubes used in offices and utilitarian fixtures, and compact fluorescents, known as CFLs, which are designed to fit the sockets of fixtures designed for traditional bulbs. These bulbs are the most energy-efficient and generally known to provide cool bright light, which washes out skin tones and looks clinical. But with improved technology, new versions have been developed to produce light in the warmer range, which is most appealing in residential settings, or to simulate the quality of daylight, which is good to use for reading.

Nowadays, many people opt for the energy-saving lightbulbs, which are usually more expensive but last longer, enabling them to more than pay for themselves over their lifetime. Remember that lower wattage CFLs produce the same level of light as much higher wattage traditional incandescent bulbs. To determine the approximate CFL equivalent to a traditional bulb, divide the wattage of the traditional bulb by 4. For a CFL wattage match to a halogen, xenon or krypton bulb, divide by 1.5. Even though technology has improved the color of light from CFLs, many people still find the quality of their light too bright and harsh for most residential applications.

ABOVE: A simple bamboo shade keeps the window looking tailored. The antique ceiling fixture was purchased by the owner in a shop in Ottawa, Canada.

TOP, LEFT: Reproduction lanterns and short pendants provide a variety of light levels in this kitchen.

BOTTOM, LEFT: Shutters over the windows in this master bedroom control light at night. A vintage chandelier and compact table lamps provide the right levels of reading light as needed.

FIXTURES

Light fixtures range from strictly utilitarian recessed can lights to highly crafted sculptural table lamps and chandeliers that can serve as decorative focal points. When choosing lighting, consider the mood you want to create and the tasks performed in the room. Then select appropriate fixtures in a style that complements your decor. Most rooms are used for multiple activities, and the right fixture can help you define zones. In a family room, for example, a reading lamp with an opaque shade placed next to a chair targets light for someone reading, while keeping the rest of the room darker for those watching television.

Integrated Fixtures

Recessed lighting These lights typically come in cylindrical housings in various sizes and are set flush with the ceiling to be relatively inconspicuous; they can provide either ambient or focused illumination. But overhead recessed downlights usually contain exposed bulbs that can cast harsh shadows on faces in a living room, are uncomfortable to look at while lying down in a bedroom and cause glare on computer screens in home offices. However, some recessed fixtures are adjustable and let you control the direction of the light beam. If you choose this type of lighting, consider aiming it at a wall to highlight art or other displayed elements in a hallway for a gallery effect. You can use warm-white CFLs or halogens for these fixtures.

Cove lighting This integrated lighting option provides more comfortable indirect light. Cove lights are typically imbedded into a soffit or built-in lip around the perimeter of a ceiling and bounce light off the ceiling. Choose linear fluorescents or xenons for this type of light.

Ceiling Fixtures

Surface- or flush-mounted fixtures These fixtures often feature dome-shaped shades that diffuse the light of a bulb and provide general ambient illumination. The best bulbs for these are traditional or warm-white CFLs.

Chandeliers Elaborate or simple, chandeliers can provide ambient illumination and they can act as a decorative focal point and inject accent sparkle. They can feature exposed bulbs or be equipped with shades that direct light up or down. Use halogen, xenon, krypton or traditional flame-shaped bulbs.

TOP: Light up in style with perforated metal pendants. The lamps cast a cheery beam where needed and also interject a spark of visual interest.

BOTTOM: A whimsical chandelier brings sparkle and drama to a dining room.

ABOVE: Make a bold statement by attaching faux blossoms to an inexpensive globe fixture with nontoxic Elmer's glue.

ABOVE, CENTER: A chandelier with uplight shades provides soft, diffuse ambient illumination.

ABOVE, RIGHT: A whimsical vintage sconce gets a modern update with new shade covers that match a grasscloth wallcovering.

Pendant lights These fixtures hang from the ceiling by a cord, rods or chains, and are equipped with globes, shades or domes that direct light up or down and often reduce glare. They can be used for general lighting when fitted with shades that direct light upward, or with globes or other shades that surround the bulbs. When fitted with shades that direct light downward, they provide task light over tables and work areas such as kitchen islands. Use CFLs to cast light on a surface a short distance away. Use traditional, halogen, xenon or krypton bulbs to illuminate surfaces more than 4 feet away.

As a general rule, chandeliers and pendant lights should hang at least 30 inches above the table to avoid harsh light in diners' eyes.

Wall-Mounted Fixtures

Sconces These fixtures are mounted on the wall, and can direct light up or down depending on the design. They can be attached to adjustable swing arms and can be topped with shades enabling them to provide focused task light. They can also be covered with simple glass or acrylic shades enabling them to shed light on a stairwell or hallway, or they can feature exposed bulbs and include mirrored and crystal accents, enabling them to provide sparkling accent light. In general, use incandescent light sources with these fixtures. Sconces with white shades will produce an unflattering light if you use a CFL.

A surface-mounted schoolhouse-
style ceiling fixture in keeping
with the style of the kitchen
provides diffuse ambient light.
A trio of pendant fixtures provides
focused downlight on the butcher-
block top of the island.

Give a simple lamp with a skinny metal base character by surrounding it with fallen sticks and branches painted white like driftwood and attached with craft glue.

TABLE AND FLOOR LAMPS

Floor lamps These fixtures provide ambient or task light, with shades that direct light up or down, and are often placed in the corners of a room. They're often designed as sculptural decorative elements, but standing floor lamps with adjustable arms cast light down to provide task or reading light. Use warm-white CFLs or incandescent sources with these lamps.

Torchieres These floor fixtures feature conical or semi-spherical shades that direct light toward the ceiling and add ambient light and drama. Use warm-white CFLs or incandescent sources with these lamps.

Table lamps They come in a vast range of styles and shapes that can add color or shapely focal points to a room while helping to provide general illumination. Use warm-white CFLs or incandescent sources with these lamps.

Reading and task lamps They often feature adjustable arms and shades that direct light onto a work or reading surface. Use 23-watt CFLs (the equivalent of a 100-watt traditional bulb) for bright light.

Under-cabinet lights These fixtures are typically installed in kitchens and attached to the base of wall-mounted cabinets to illuminate a counter surface below. Use incandescent xenon or krypton bulbs (not halogen; it's too hot) to light natural stone surfaces; use warm-white linear CFLs or LED strips to light matte laminate surfaces.

Accent and picture lights Small integrated LEDs or halogens in cabinets and bookshelves showcase decorative ceramics or vases. Ceiling-mounted track lights or accent lights recessed into the ceiling, as well as picture lights, which can be attached to the wall directly above a picture frame, highlight art, tapestries or wall-mounted displays. Low-voltage halogens are best for these fixtures as they render the full range of the color spectrum extremely well.

SHADES AND CONTROLS

Lampshades can help you control light. The shape, material and opacity of the shade will all affect the direction and the quality of the light, by sending the light up or down, impacting the color, and diffusing it to create sparkle or reduce glare.

Putting lights on dimmers gives you even more control over brightness and mood. While you can put individual fixtures on dimmers, integrated dimming systems let you control the lighting in an entire room with one switch. Some allow you to preset different lighting "scenes" for different times of day or activities.

Dimmers also help you to conserve energy and extend the life of your bulbs. The Skylark Eco-Dim dimmer from Lutron Electronics, for example, is programmed to limit light levels to no more than 85 percent of full capacity at all times. The decrease in light level is imperceptible to the eye, but can reduce energy usage by 15 percent—more than doubling the life of an incandescent bulb.

BELOW, LEFT: It's easy to turn an old vessel—such as a large glass bottle, ginger jar or teapot—into a lamp with a lamp-making kit available at crafts or hardware stores.

BELOW: Small energy-efficient light fixtures integrated into the tops of the cabinetry keep the glass-fronted portions bright in this small kitchen.

QUICK FIXES
Room Brighteners

COUNTRY CHIC Give an old lamp a second chance with a new shade and a fresh coat of paint. To make this one, we took a cheerful yellow gingham, starched and ironed it to make the pleats, and then glued it onto a plain shade. Yellow ribbons at the top and bottom hide the raw edges.

ROPE TWIST Two colors of twine wrapped around and glued to the shade of this small sconce give it a bold yet earthy appeal suitable for its nautical setting.

LIGHTEN UP

Brighten your kitchen and bath without breaking the bank by using a few of these simple updates:

- Add some polish with light-reflecting surfaces: glossy white walls, stainless steel appliances and chrome fixtures.

- Rejuvenate timeworn furnishings with a couple of coats of pristine white enamel or glossy cream paint.

- Change dated countertops to a light-colored laminate or pale-colored solid surface material.

- Look to pale floor tiles to keep a snug room feeling open. Or refinish an existing wood floor to banish dinginess.

- Swap cabinet door insets for glass.

- Spotlight counters with under-cabinet strip lights. And highlight an island or worktable with mini-pendants. For extra sparkle, search out a flea-market chandelier.

- Leave tops of windows bare or use sheer curtains and shades.

BERIBBONED BEAUTY Random strips of grosgrain ribbon glued around the face of a lampshade add a touch of whimsy.

SHELLED OUT Gathered from the seashore, souvenir shells can be put to decorative use when attached with Elmer's glue to the paper shade of a simple sconce.

Clutter
Control

A built-in armoire next to the fireplace in this living room gracefully conceals a flat-screen TV and other paraphernalia when they're not in use.

ORGANIZING EVERY ROOM OF THE HOUSE

The palette in your room may be perfect and its furnishings beautiful, but even a small pocket of clutter can destroy its appeal. The flotsam and jetsam of daily life has a way of creeping into every room—and managing it can challenge the most fanatic of neatniks. But controlling clutter and keeping your rooms neat and organized will vastly increase your odds of closing a deal if you want to sell your home, and greatly improve the quality of your life if you want to keep it.

To stow your stuff with style, start by taking the time to review each room and put some pointers from professional organizers into practice. Most suggest starting with a good purge. Then make the most of the ever-growing array of storage elements—from built-in cabinets and closet systems to freestanding armoires, sideboards and trunks to shelves, plate racks, peg rails and baskets—to help you corral the possessions you need to keep, but not necessarily in plain sight.

Mudrooms

If any room has the potential to pile up with a jumble of coats, hats, boots and other gear, it's the mudroom—the first room a potential buyer or your family members are likely to see when they walk in. To be sure this room presents an appealing picture, try following any of these tips:

Think seasonally If it's winter, there is no need for summer essentials to be in the mudroom, and vice versa. Store out-of-season items elsewhere.

Give everyone their due Allot an area, hook or cubby for each person in the household. Don't forget the furry family members—they, too, need a spot for accessories such as leashes, toys and towels.

Consider the bigger picture Choose storage items designed to hold what you need to stow. If you live in a cold climate, you may need more than just a few hooks for outerwear. If there's a place for everything, it's more likely to be put away.

Talk to each other Hang a mail slot, a message board to create a spot for family notes, and a calendar.

BELOW: Provide a repository for keys, mail, gloves and pocketbooks. The classic hall stand keeps everything neat as well as offers a spot to sit.

OPPOSITE, TOP: A mix of door styles and staggered height on cabinets provide a farmhouse-y, furniturelike feel in this kitchen.

OPPOSITE, BOTTOM: Cabinets and drawers in a variety of sizes maximize storage.

Kitchens

To get your cooking space into working order, start by getting rid of bulky appliances that you rarely use. They quickly eat up valuable counter surfaces. Then narrow down items further by examining what you use on a daily, weekly and monthly basis. This will help determine which items to keep close at hand and which to stow elsewhere or eliminate altogether.

Then ask yourself what is working and what isn't. Bring in a friend or family member for feedback or helpful suggestions. Everybody benefits from an outside perspective. Once you've cleared the kitchen, follow up with daily maintenance to ensure that things won't get out of control later. For more help with keeping your kitchen clutter under control, consider these additional professional organizing tips:

Stay focused Concentrate on the kitchen's primary purpose, to nourish the family. If too many other things are going on in the room, it becomes a magnet for clutter. Keep the tabletop clear for family dinners.

Use it or lose it Try the one-month cardboard box test. Put all gadgets, small appliances and utensils in a box on the counter. If you use an item from the box, put it back in your drawers. Whatever is left in the box for a month, you probably do not need.

Go deep Take advantage of every inch with organizational aids. Use a lazy Susan, mini–step shelves, racks and even back-of-door shelving systems to hold items and provide a clear view of what you're storing. Deep drawers allow you to store lots of things but still see what you have. Look for items that nest well together to expand your storage space.

Limit design elements Cooking accessories can stay out on a counter if they tie in with one or two main design elements like a stainless steel fridge and dishwasher.

Customize when necessary If a standard island won't fit in your kitchen, have a restaurant supply store make a narrow table that is both affordable and fits the space.

Hide little-used items Use the upper-cabinet, hard-to-reach spaces for things you only use once in a while. Place them on lazy Susans so you can see what's stored in the back.

Maximize your space Turn a broom closet into a pantry—better to have pasta sauce on hand when you need it than a mop you use occasionally. Store attractive cooking utensils like a mallet and rolling pin in an old ceramic pot on a wall shelf nearby. Nest containers or bowls to save space. If you have plastic containers, store lids vertically near their match and toss any with missing lids or those not meant for microwaves. Take advantage of vertical space for a cookware stand, hanging shelves or spice racks.

Designate a spot for recyclables Use totes big enough to hold a few days' worth of recyclables but light enough to carry when full.

Make a list of your family's staples and favorite meals, and keep those key ingredients stocked—but not overstocked.

Bathrooms

According to some professional organizers, clutter in the bathroom would not be an issue for most people if they kept only what they used. If you haven't used a product in over a year, chances are you don't need it and won't ever use it.

To ensure a beautifully organized bath, try these additional professional organizing tips:

Assign a place for everything To make sure things get put back, store them near where you use them most.

Use attractive containers to help add visual appeal to the environment while keeping things organized.

Take advantage of wall space with decorative shelves, hooks or wall ladders.

Divide and conquer Group all of your products according to how they're used: showering, shaving, makeup application and removal, and hair styling. Keep each collection in its own container and it will be easy to retrieve what you need.

Organize your kids Assign a different color towel and washcloth to each child so it will be obvious which one belongs to whom. Carry the theme through to toothbrushes and water cups.

Make cleaning convenient If it's easy to keep clean, it will stay organized, too. Stash one complete set of cleaning products in each bathroom. It will be a cinch to disinfect the area when you have a few spare minutes.

Waste not Make the most of every inch, especially in a small bath. Stack woven baskets in the space under a pedestal sink. Purchase a freestanding unit that straddles the toilet tank and has open shelves or a closed cabinet above.

Look for hidden storage space Streamline the bathroom by making use of wasted space on the back of the door. It's the perfect place to hang a fabric shoe holder that can keep hair dryers, curling irons and spare toiletries out of the way.

A new spin Try a simple two-level turntable inside your bathroom cabinets. It will give you easy access to lotions, hairspray and more.

Make it clear Acrylic caddies let you quickly see everything at a glance, while the individual compartments keep items neat.

The great divide Use expandable drawer dividers that organize items of all sizes.

Get it together Group like items together in your cabinets to locate them more easily and keep frequently used items at eye level.

ABOVE: Furniturelike cabinets and drawers turn this bath into an inviting and practical retreat.

BELOW: Built-ins beneath the windows provide his-and-hers storage in this compact bath—with just enough room for a mini-vanity in between.

Bedrooms

The bedroom should be a peaceful oasis, but as the final destination at the end of a long day, it can often be the repository of heaps of worn clothing, shopping bags, portable technology gadgets or cast-off slippers. Consider these tips to keep the bedroom tidy:

Stay relaxed Find another place for things such as laptops, cell phones and anything else that might hinder your ability to unwind.

Make your bed It may seem like a small thing, but the bed anchors the room and sets the tone for the entire space. If your bed is a rumpled mess, your bedroom probably will be, too.

Invest in a hamper Get into the habit of placing dirty clothes into a hamper as soon as you take them off. This keeps the floor clear of clutter and all your laundry in one place, ready to be washed.

Take stock If you haven't worn something in a year, donate it to charity. This includes bargain purchases that still have the original sales tags, clothes that don't fit and duplicates.

The shelving in this guest room showcases a few of the owner's favorite flea-market finds—kitschy 1950s novels, along with souvenirs and fabric-covered boxes—just like in an old bed-and-breakfast.

A slab of laminate atop mobile metal cabinets provides a desk with storage in the loft bedroom of this beach house. Pull-out drawers beneath the bed provide an additional spot to stow bedding.

Home Offices

When it comes to clearing out a mess in the home office, you've got to mean business. Consider these tips for restoring order in this hard-to-keep-clean space:

Stop the paper trail Since approximately 80 percent of daily mail is junk, a shredder is a great investment to help eliminate paper clutter and make the remaining 20 percent manageable.

Make it pretty If your desk is uninviting and cluttered, you aren't going to want to sit there. Personalize the area with items like a favorite vase or glass used as a pencil holder.

Save or purge Check with your accountant about what important papers need to be filed and for how long. Once a year, set a date to shred and toss outdated files.

Save or splurge Shop dollar stores and flea markets for bargain baskets, bins and desk accessories. Use your budget for more expensive buys, such as closet systems.

Living Rooms and Dining Rooms

Clutter may be a bit less likely to accumulate in living rooms and dining spaces, but piles of newspapers and magazines or collections of kids' stuff can easily find their way into these spaces. Storage furniture—from coffee tables with drawers and shelves and ottomans that open up for stowing throws in the living room to sideboards and corner hutches for housing dishes and table linens in the dining room—can add both function and beauty to these rooms. Built-in entertainment units or bookshelves can add purpose-driven architectural character, too.

LEFT: An overscale hutch anchors this small dining room, providing storage for linens and display space for an attractive collection of china.

ABOVE: A reproduction map chest serves as a coffee table and adds a nautical feeling. Above the fireplace, paneled wood doors mask the TV.

BUILT-IN CABINETS, DRAWERS AND CLOSETS

Built-in Cabinets

Built-in cabinets not only can help you add highly prized functional storage space, but, like paneling and millwork elements, they will also add aesthetic and dollar value to your home. Virtually every home has pockets of unused real estate—space beneath staircases, areas flanking fireplaces, niches near windows—where built-in storage areas can add charm and function.

If you can afford to hire a millwork specialist or carpenter to build in a window seat with pullout drawers or a lift-top seat, or install built-in cabinets or integrated cupboards with custom millwork, you can make the most of every square inch of your home and enhance its architectural character at the same time. But even if you're not in a position to splurge on custom built-ins, you can install ready-made shelves next to a fireplace, for example, and make them look built-in by adding crown and base molding and doors that tie in with other architectural features in your home. Or you can build up existing molding with cost-effective trim, or add an instant feeling of history by adding raised-panel doors.

In a compact kitchen where existing cabinets don't reach the ceiling, you might install new cabinets that climb all the way up. Or you could add new, glass-fronted doors, painted to match the originals, atop existing cabinets to add functional storage space while keeping a sense of airiness. Pull-out spice pantries squeezed beneath the cooktop or in a narrow space between a refrigerator and stove help corral similar staples in one spot while providing easy access. Add a unique knob or drawer pull in a similar material to other hardware to accent special drawers or cabinets. Deep drawers in base cabinets are ideal for storing cookware. Utensils and flatware can be stashed in the drawers above them.

Companies that specialize in designing and creating built-in closets and storage spaces, such as California Closets, can provide design consultation advice and install storage systems custom-suited to your needs to maximize every square inch of available space for an average cost of around $2,500 to $3,000. Such units are value-added upgrades that can serve as selling points for prospective buyers, or as flexible spaces that can adapt to changing needs as family members move through various life stages. A built-in nursery closet, for example, can be adapted with adjustable rods and shelves to accommodate the needs of a teen as a child grows. Or a media center storage space can double as a home office zone, attractively concealing electronic equipment.

OPPOSITE, TOP: Beautiful raised-panel cabinets, built of glazed knotty pine (a mellow wood favored in kitchens in the south of France), give this new kitchen an antique look. Some cabinet doors are faced with chicken wire, enabling pretty kitchen pieces to be displayed. Drawers and slim pull-out spice cabinets provide additional practical storage.

OPPOSITE, BOTTOM: Built-in bookcases on either side of the fireplace feature recessed-panel doors that match the Federal-style architecture, cleverly concealing essentials of modern living such as a flat-screen TV.

KITCHEN STORAGE IDEAS

Make every inch count with some of these creative, and sometimes frugal, storage ideas:

- A built-in wine rack *(top, left)* is an efficient way to keep a variety of favorite vintages on hand but out of the way. To pump up efficiency, stash corkscrews and glasses in drawers nearby.

- A pull-out bin next to the stove *(top, right)* makes it easy to toss trash but doesn't gobble up floor space. The result? More room for traffic to flow. Glass canisters hold supplies like sugar and pasta at the ready, while also adding a subtle decorative touch.

- Kudos to the inventor of the magnetic knife holder! Knives are always ready when the cook needs them *(bottom, left)*. Plant utensils in a sturdy container so they're easy to reach and organized, too. Choose a holder—such as a crock or ceramic vase—that echoes your scheme.

- A pull-out pantry *(bottom, right)*, 24 inches deep, makes good use of a wedge of space beside the range. The cook can stir a pot and reach for paprika at the same time.

Clothing Closets

The average person cleans out his or her closet only every two to five years. That's a lot of time for clutter to accumulate! To get past the paralysis that the prospect of clearing a closet can cause, many pros suggest taking on the task in baby steps to keep it from feeling so daunting.

Try setting a timer for 10 minutes, then go through as much as you can in that time. Begin on one end of your closet and pull out items that can be given away, folded instead of hung, or stored elsewhere for the season. Depending on your progress, when the time is up, you can either reset for another 10 minutes and keep going, or start again later. You may need a few rounds to finish.

Once you've weeded out extraneous clothing, take a look at what's left and think about how best to organize it. Investing in a system like the one pictured here will help you maximize storage. One of the biggest problems people have is that they look at the floor space rather than valuable wall space. Instead, think vertically. Create two short hanging spaces instead of one long one to double your hanging space. Remember, you can fit more into an organized closet than a cluttered one.

Consider the following additional tips for keeping your clothing closet tidy, once and for all:

Rein in stacks Folded clothing can get messy quickly, so keep casual pieces in baskets or bins that you can pull off the shelf, or stow them in stackable boxes, which allow you to make better use of vertical space. Slide-out wire drawers keep purses visible and easy to grab. If you like to match your purse with your belt, store perfect pairs together.

Divide your closet into zones One area should be dedicated to items used every day, one to those used occasionally, and the last to those used infrequently. Your everyday items should be most accessible—between waist and eye level.

Shelve it Reserve high shelves for infrequently used items, like special-occasion accessories or cold-weather layers. The highest shelf should be no more than 6 feet 3 inches from the floor or the average person will need a stepladder to reach it.

Keep valuables hidden Drawers are great for storing small items or jewelry. If you're storing disparate items in a drawer, use organizers to keep the bottom of the drawer from becoming the "ignore pile." Stow jewelry and accessories in boxes or inside cabinet doors, where they'll be safe from dust and out of children's reach. A shallow tray can corral small frequently used items, such as watches, everyday earrings or sunglasses.

ABOVE AND OPPOSITE: Customized clothing closets developed by California Closets include shelves, niches, slots with hanging rods, and drawers, which accommodate shoes, bags, jewelry and belts, as well as hung and folded clothing.

Make use of space down under You're more likely to wear all of your shoes if you can see them and don't have to search for pairs. Store them in clear shoe drawers at the bottom of your closet or place them side by side on shoe racks, which can be stacked to hold multiple pairs of shoes.

Hang it up Don't fill your closet with wire hangers from the dry cleaner—the thin metal can leave wrinkle marks or rust stains. The average woman needs a few different kinds of hangers or a multifunction hanger. A wooden or foam hanger with indented shoulder sections and a cross bar with clips will accommodate suits, shirts, pants and skirts.

FURNITURE AND CONTAINER STORAGE

Just because your clutter is an eyesore doesn't mean the container or unit it's stowed in has to be. Instead of stashing stuff in plastic bins or unattractive boxes, consider adding style and function to your decor with any of the many multipurpose furniture pieces available with creative integrated storage options. Manufacturers now make all kinds of double-duty furnishings, such as beds with built-in drawers; mini-bar units that open up into serving stations with housing for bottles, linens and stemware, then fold away into sleek cabinets; or ottomans that open up with storage space for seasonal cushions and throws.

From tables with drawers to armoires with shelves and drawers to entertainment units with cubbies and doors, storage furniture should be selected as much for its style as its function and should harmonize with the other furnishings in your rooms.

You can also transform existing pieces into storage elements. Place a floor-length table topper over a hall table and stow boots or umbrellas below, or add a skirt to a nightstand as a way to hide books or reading glasses. Or give an old element, such as a shutter, new purpose as a wall-mounted storage piece for notes, mail, keys and other daily paraphernalia.

Any number of beautiful containers, such as woven baskets, leather magazine holders or fabric-covered boxes, can also enhance your decor while adding function. Stacked next to chairs, covered boxes or baskets can double as side tables or nightstands. Think of elements like these as decorative accents as well as catchalls. They can add texture, color, pattern and sculptural form to a room.

TOP: A country-style painted armoire opens up to reveal a computer station, complete with slide-out keyboard tray and shelves for the printer and other attachments.

BOTTOM: The vintage pine hutch in this dining room displays the owner's collection of blue-and-white English transferware, along with new and old pieces she has collected.

REPURPOSED SPACE SAVERS

Save money by repurposing existing furniture and accents or reclaiming someone else's castoffs as affordable storage devices.

- Place a tag-sale toy chest or an inexpensive bench with a lift-up top beneath a window or at the foot of a bed. Stash seldom-used items or blankets inside.

- Turn attractive recycled food or beverage containers into caddies for utensils; unify them by painting them the same color.

- Collect vintage baskets to house lightweight items like linens and paper goods. Stage an artful array of them atop the cabinets or on bookshelves.

- Recycle a stepladder or stool from the past. Stack the tiered steps with cookbooks, plants or piles of colorful vintage tablecloths or quilts.

- Put out a tray. Instead of letting them roam, group together items you use every day, like salt and pepper shakers, or the sugar bowl and creamer. Choose a wood, metal or rattan tray according to your decorating theme.

- Recruit a yard-sale sideboard or cupboard to stash extra dishes, small appliances or special baking pans.

- Use a piece of attractive crockery or silver bucket to contain necessities in style. Search consignment shops and antiques markets for decorative accessories that complement your theme in color and style. Recycled creamers, vases and sugar bowls can become fanciful containers for brushes, soaps and sponges.

Urns—in all their lovely variations—are spectacular sculptural storage pieces. Use them to hold linens and utensils, serve as bookends, house magazines or contain paperclips and pushpins.

SHELVES, RACKS AND PEG RAILS

Just as all homes have hidden zones with storage potential for custom built-ins, they also invariably contain swaths of wall space. These can afford ideal spots for bracketed or surface-mounted shelves, plate racks, peg rails and hooks that can allow you to make use of vertical space for storage of practical yet visually appealing items, such as porcelain plates, pitchers, books, hats and other items that can be stowed in the open. With just a little creativity you can make the most of wall space—and ban the clutter—once and for all.

Fireplaces, for example, usually protrude up to a foot or more from the wall, which makes the space on either side perfect for built-in shelves. For aesthetic appeal, vary the types of objects on the shelves, and stagger the placement of the items to avoid an overly uniform look.

In a kitchen you can give your everyday dishes some breathing room by getting them out of the cabinets and stowing teacups or mugs on hooks mounted below cabinets. Or free up valuable counter space by creating a baking center on the wall of a tucked-away area, such as the space beneath a staircase. The diagonal line of the stair creates a triangular alcove ideal for shelves, a towel rack and hooks.

You might also line a pass-through between a kitchen and dining area with shelves. Or, you could wind a narrow shelf around the kitchen or dining room's perimeter near the ceiling to show off antique bottles and pitchers. Shelves mounted on the end of an island make a fine perch for cookbooks.

STOW SIMPLE

- Increase the width of a windowsill: Add a narrow shelf mounted on brackets in front of the sill. Fill the new platform with sun-loving plants like geraniums.

- Add a bottom shelf to a kitchen worktable for stacking colorful mixing bowls and oversize platters.

- Turn a range hood into a showcase with a display shelf for favorite plates or platters. To add even more architectural character, screw or glue drapery finials onto wood supports.

- Install a narrow shelf across a window to store and display vintage glassware or a collection of shapely vases or pitchers and make space in cabinets for less attractive items.

- Hang Shaker pegs along one wall to corral everyday coats and prevent a jumbled mess. Shelves can hold baskets of gloves, scarves and outdoor paraphernalia.

- Free up drawers by using an expandable, wall-mounted towel rack to hold dishcloths, Shaker pegs for utensils, and hooks for pots and pans.

- Purchase or recycle a metal clip-rack to hang up grocery lists, invitations and mail, or to post schedules and messages.

ABOVE, LEFT: The chocolate-colored walls in this home office set off a display of light-hued ceramics and vases on modern built-in shelves. The bird's-eye maple desk with its flush drawers interprets a mid-20th-century modern piece.

ABOVE, RIGHT: The brick wall in this sitting room contrasts with the white shelves and provides a textured background for the pieces on display. The objects on the shelves are varied for a more pleasing look: books on one, decorative objects on another, baskets on a third.

LEFT: A tin picnic basket stores mittens and scarves in winter, flip-flops in summer. Hooks beneath the plate rail provide easily accessible spots for stowing bags and jackets.

OPPOSITE, TOP: Old apothecary jars and flowerpots hold a variety of knickknacks to keep this mudroom neat and tidy. An antique wire basket organizes a collection of contemporary balls, while cheery vintage paintings add color and character to the space.

OPPOSITE, BOTTOM: Construct a skinny shelf to take advantage of a nook beneath cabinets. Such roosts make ideal homes for everyday supplies like spices. For added charm, transfer spices into fetching tag-sale-bought canisters.

QUICK FIXES

EASY ACCESS Use pretty brackets to hang a simple shelf made of galvanized steel for a potting bench to hold favorite cooking ingredients and small pots of homegrown herbs as well as art.

SPICE CAROUSEL Use a lazy Susan to organize spices and supplies. Search flea markets and consignment stores for a model that fits your counter. Or build your own tiered tray using lazy Susan hardware available at hardware stores.

CLEVER CATCHALL Press a vintage bamboo planter or a metal baker's rack into service as a catchall for kitchenware—from breadboards and platters to fruit bowls and buckets. Stow a basket below for extra storage.

DISPLAY CHINA
Construct or purchase a plate rack to display favorite china. Paint or stain it to match your decor. To heighten the drama, create an eye-catching vignette by including a pretty dishtowel or two and an interesting tag sale urn to hold utensils.

Focal Points

A room can be thoughtfully laid out and filled with beautiful furnishings, but without the finishing touches it can lack vitality. Paintings, sculptures, photographs and collectibles—when thoughtfully selected and placed—can inject personality into a room and bring it to life. A stunning portrait can command attention over a fireplace mantel, a collection of transferware platters can keep the eye moving around a plate rack encircling a room, a thoughtful tableau of earthenware vessels on a small table can enliven an empty corner. The value of these focal points lies not so much in their provenance or price, but in their ability to spark energy and evoke emotion.

Art and collectibles not only afford you an opportunity to add interest to bare walls or introduce depth and dimension to an arrangement of furniture, they also enable you to express your personal style. So the most compelling pieces are those that have meaning to you—either historically or personally—and resonate within the context of your rooms and furnishings, especially if you plan to keep your home. But even if you want to sell it, well-edited, well-placed artworks or pleasingly presented collectibles can help a prospective buyer envision the potential spirit of a room enlivened with his or her own personal touches.

When a staircase becomes the defining element that separates public and private spaces, art can aid in emphasizing the distinction. The lower, more formal area features a single framed traditional painting. Mounted asymmetrically, a collection of black-and-white photographs on the side wall above reflects the personality of the collector/artist. White mats and black frames unify the disparate shapes and subjects of the photographs.

ART

If you're fortunate enough to have deep pockets and a good eye—or a good art adviser—then you may opt to enrich your rooms with works of fine art by old masters or promising contemporary artists. But even if your budget is limited, you can still make a statement with art by trolling flea markets or Internet auctions for bargains, or framing children's drawings or your own Sunday watercolors. Either way, honing in on a genre, period, or style of art can help you fine-tune a visual point of view and establish a sense of continuity within a room—or from room to room. Doing so also enables you to deepen your understanding of a particular area of art and sharpen your eye to quality.

You might, for example, limit the art you collect to serene landscapes, 20th-century Minimalist paintings, or contemporary black-and-white photographs. Or you could collect Dutch still-life paintings, 1930s movie posters, or botanical prints. Choosing works of art that contrast with the style of your furnishings—pairing a Roy Lichtenstein lithograph with traditional furnishings, for example—can add vitality to a room, as long as there's a continuous point of reference among your different works of art. But the style of your furnishings and your rooms will set the tone for kinds of art that will work in the space. Formal rooms with furnishings upholstered in velvet or silk need art with a refined sensibility, for example, while country-style rooms are ideal for flea-market folk art finds.

Although the colors and imagery in a work of art needn't match your furnishings, they shouldn't fight with them, either. Keep in mind the scale of the artwork in relation to the wall space or the furnishings nearby, too. By the same token, the size and shape of sculptural pieces needs to harmoniously relate to the other three-dimensional elements—and to the proportions of the room itself. If you're trying to sell your home, now's the time to review the art you have—and edit if need be—to showcase the works and the rooms they occupy in their best light.

TOP: Eileen Kathryn Boyd, the designer of this cheerful sitting room, created the dramatic flower painting herself, using the print of a favorite blouse as her inspiration. The artwork also determined the color scheme for the room.

BOTTOM: The step-style placement of this collection of artwork reinforces the lines of the staircase. Unified by the same style and color of frames and similar mats, the works also harmonize with the spirit of the space. This collage is a creative way to utilize a narrow setting for art. The little mirror in the ornate frame adds visual interest and depth.

OPPOSITE: A symmetrical trio of woodland scenes, centered by the largest work, gives a casual look and feel to a Craftsman-inspired living room.

Framing and Displaying Art

The way in which a work of art is framed and displayed will play a strong role in how it's perceived. Consider, for example, the impact a collection of miniature drawings can make when surrounded by large mats and displayed as a group. A large-scale piece of Pop Art, on the other hand, needs plenty of breathing room and furnishings that can stand up to it without competing for attention, while an atmospheric landscape mounted in a simple frame over a headboard can enhance the spirit of serenity in a bedroom.

Containing fallen leaves, fronds and flower petals, gilded frames in various shapes and sizes are grouped together to make an artistic statement in and of themselves.

PROPER FRAMES

When it comes to framing a work of art, there are no hard-and-fast rules, but following some basic hanging and framing techniques will enable you to showcase your artwork to its advantage. To bring out the best in your art, apply these tips on framing and matting:

Consider the context as well as the artwork Each framing decision is individual. The frames, or what professionals call moldings, can either complement or contrast with the artworks, depending on the time period, style and artist's intent.

Enhance a photo or work on paper with a mat Although it's not always necessary to use mats, doing so can often provide a dramatic effect. For example, an overscale mat around a tiny image can help draw attention to the artwork as a stand-alone piece and increase its perceived scale in relation to other elements in a room. It can also lend weight and drama to a collection of similar small-scale pieces.

Use archival-quality products Acid-free materials are standard and available at any frame shop. They should be used on all works to protect them from chemical damage and discoloration.

Protect photographs, textiles and fragile works on paper from harmful sunlight
Light-filtering glass is a must, but avoid "low-glare" glass, which distorts and dulls the image. You can also apply film to the windows or the glass in front to block ultraviolet rays.

PERFECT PLACEMENT

Placing your art properly will enable it to get the attention it deserves. The right spot for a work of art depends not only on the available wall, floor or table space, but also on the size and color of the framed work in relation to other furnishings. A big room will look disproportionately large, for example, if its walls feature tiny works of art. Furthermore, a lot of small pieces poorly displayed can look like clutter rather than points of interest. For large walls with little detail or trim work, try a grouping of nicely framed art or one grand framed piece. Sight lines and circulation paths through a room will also come into play.

To further show off your art to best advantage, try these additional tips on mounting and placing it like a pro:

Follow the golden rule of hanging art Mount the work so that its center is 60 inches from the floor. It's acceptable, however, to break this rule in certain spaces. In children's rooms, for example, art should be placed lower for easy viewing.

Explore your options Try out the artwork in several places before hanging permanently to see how it looks in changing light. If possible, enlist an artist or dealer friend to help select the proper spot.

Plan in advance If you want to arrange a collection of works in a grouping, lay the pieces out on the floor first to see how they look, or make templates from paper in the exact sizes of each work and hang the templates on the wall with painter's tape to visualize the placement.

Keep it clean Wear gloves when hanging so the oil from your hands doesn't mar the finish of the frame.

Do your hardware homework Choose a hanger that is stronger than recommended for the weight of your work, and use a plastic-coated wire hanger to prevent fraying. Also, select hardware that is appropriate for the walls; there are specific hangers and nails for brick, Sheetrock and plaster.

Try something unpredictable New York designer Jamie Drake likes to display art in ways that add to the composition of a vignette while enhancing the viewing experience of the art itself. A small detailed piece placed on a small easel on an end table, for example, will glow in the light cast by a table lamp. Or try hanging a bold piece above an armoire or media cabinet to create a feeling of greater height, and place a vase, urn or sculpture to the side in front of it.

MAKE YOUR OWN NATURE-INSPIRED WORKS OF ART

- Blow up photographs of favorite flowers, outdoor scenes or weather events to hang on a family-room wall. To add even more interest, cut the enlargement in sections and hang them separately as a triptych.
- Use a flower press to dry leaves and ferns. Attach them to card stock and frame. A multiple display adds a surprisingly graphic punch to a simple shelf arrangement.
- Copy landscape plans from garden books and use them to paper a wall.
- Accessorize with garden-inspired items. Frame vintage seed packets or pages from an old book of botanical drawings.

COLLECTIONS

The urge to collect runs deep. And the thrill of hunting for treasures is matched only by gathering your finds into an artful assemblage. Virtually anything—teapots, seashells, Appalachian baskets or African wood carvings—becomes more interesting when displayed in groups. The key is to present your cherished objects in a context that suits their inherent spirit. You wouldn't display a collection of watering cans in a formal room, for example, but you could make a neat row of seashells feel completely at home on a windowsill in a beach house.

Though some experts say the cardinal rule for collectors is to buy what you love, others are adamant about collecting elements that are as useful as they are beautiful. For many of us, space is too precious to save things we'll never use. Why not tote around some of the straw handbags of a collection that adds texture to your bedroom wall? Or how about storing your china or ceramic pieces out in the open in easily accessible areas in order to make using them more convenient? Charming tea sets, pretty plates, interesting soup tureens and impressive platters can be stunning when artfully displayed.

Collections of objects can enable you to add color and pattern to walls, sculptural form and dimension to tables and surfaces, and pops of interest and visual relief amid books on shelves. Whether you're feathering your nest to keep or staging it to sell, your collections can be one of the most powerful tools for enlivening your rooms with a dramatic and very personal focus of attention. The more personal your home, the happier you'll be living in it—and the more welcoming it will be to friends and visitors.

BELOW, LEFT: Color unifies this tableau of contrasting things—cherished photos in painted driftwood frames, fluffy flowers next to a trinket box made of jagged shells, polished marble talismans and a mother-of-pearl lamp.

BELOW, CENTER: A motley mix of old mirrors felicitously commingles in a symmetrical arrangement over a dining room sideboard.

BELOW, RIGHT: A large collection of shell crafts, starfish and other seaside mementos gets prime placement on the table in a foyer.

OPPOSITE: White is soothing, especially if a collection is large. Turn an entire wall into a panorama of flea-market finds and hand-thrown ceramics, unified by organic shapes and a streamlined palette. Painting walls and shelves white and bookending the display with polished woods, baskets, mercury glass and pewter makes it look elegant, not busy.

Arranging Advice

No matter what you collect, when it comes to displaying it, your number-one goal should be to coalesce the individual pieces into beautiful tableaux rather than scatter them about like so much clutter. The first step is to collect pieces that harmonize with the character of your rooms or furnishings. You might hunt for vintage breadboards to mount on the wall of a country kitchen, for example, or choreograph a changing display of crystal candlesticks in a lighted curio cabinet.

Always find a unifying thread to link your objects together. You might collect porcelain pieces from China, the Netherlands, England and Mexico but unify them by choosing only pieces that are blue and white. You could let the shape of an object—such as slim juggling pins or circular cake molds—dictate your groupings. Or you might hone in on a certain type of piece—such as transferware or yellowware ceramics.

To create a cohesive effect, avoid mixing elements that contrast in spirit, unless you can tie them together with a unifying device, such as color. For instance, you might place a sun-washed seashell next to a collection of mother-of-pearl boxes. Another helpful organizing tool is the use of symmetry. But don't be afraid to break a rigorous line for impact. Too much balance can bore the eye. Move objects about and edit or add to them to keep your arrangements fresh.

When arranged as well-edited tablescapes, mounted on walls, or peppered throughout a bookshelf, three-dimensional objects come to life. Just be sure their visual weight is balanced. Tablescapes or small vignettes afford you an opportunity to tell a story or create a narrative. In a vignette of three objects, you might introduce an element of surprise by setting off two like objects with an unexpected counterpoint. One final rule of thumb: Since family photographs are so very personal, display them on shelves, tables or walls in your home's more private spaces, such as bedrooms, home offices or dens.

ABOVE: A collection of vintage flour and sugar canisters takes pride of place on a plate rail around a family room.

OPPOSITE, TOP: An array of plates in preppy pink and lime green hues and multiple patterns provides a fetching focal point on a dining room wall.

OPPOSITE, BOTTOM: The floral motifs of blue-and-white platters, soup tureens, creamers and teapots contrast with the warm brown-and-blue striped upholstery fabric on the banquette in this sunny breakfast nook.

DISH IT UP

Ceramic and porcelain plates, pitchers, tureens and teacups are among the most popular pieces to collect. Here are a few ways to display them:

■ **Corral a collection** Cover an entire wall with an attractive arrangement of plates; parade a group of teapots atop kitchen cabinets; or show off mugs, bowls and serving pieces on the open shelves of a Welsh cupboard.

■ **Create a lineup** Arrange pitchers on shelves that circle the perimeter of the kitchen. Perch creamers on glass shelves installed in front of a window.

■ **Ring a room or doorway** Install a plate rail in a kitchen or dining room and top it with a frieze of plates. Frame a bedroom doorway with a collection of hand-painted floral plates. Encircle a bathroom with a chair rail of small commemorative dishes.

■ **Notice the niches** Fill niches flanking a sofa with a collection of pretty plates on plate holders. Set off a corner in a study or library with a dramatic coat of paint and fill it with an arrangement of export china.

■ **Stack them up** Use a graduated wrought-iron plate stand to stack a collection of hotel china or ceramic washbowls.

■ **Look up** Emphasize architectural features with your china or ceramic pieces. Heighten the effect of a cathedral ceiling with a triangular tableau of creamware or Spode dinnerware. Display a funky enamel platter over a kitchen door. Decorate a stove hood with souvenir plates from cafes.

■ **Set a table** Place all the makings for a proper tea party on a tray in the living room. Tea for two with all the accoutrements provides both visual pleasure and a warm welcome for guests. Arrange a breakfast table with colorful Quimper pottery. Accommodate houseguests with a bed tray holding mugs for morning coffee.

■ **Fill them up** Use pitchers to hold masses of flowers throughout the house; float single blooms in soup bowls as a centerpiece; fill washbowls with apples, skeins of wool or grapevine balls; top tiered cake plates with sweets, fruits and flowers.

■ **Be inventive** Create a montage of favorite pieces on a mantel. Prop plates on easels among an assemblage of books and figurines. Place plates on stands in bookshelves to break up a dense expanse of books. Choose ones with motifs that reflect the subjects of the books: sporting scenes in front of outdoor books, culinary themes for cookbooks, floral plates in front of gardening tomes.

■ **Salvage chipped or cracked favorite shards** Even broken plates can bring pleasure. Apply glue to the backs of broken bits of dishes or ceramic tiles and press them onto the surface of an old piece of furniture to create a pleasing design. Fill in the spaces between the shards with grout. After the grout has set, wash off residue. Tabletops are ambitious projects, but picture frames, trivets and vases are achievable goals for most amateurs. Or use Super Glue to attach a mirror cut to the appropriate shape into the center of a cracked platter. Or turn an unmatched plate into a clock: Drill a small hole into the middle of the plate, attach clockworks and hang to keep everyone on time for dinner.

FIREPLACES

A hearth has always been the heart of a home. Whether your fireplace is utilitarian and made of basic bricks, streamlined with a sleek surround, or grand and topped with a marble mantel, it's the built-in centerpiece in any room it occupies. Make the most of it by playing up its assets with your art or collections. Call attention to a graceful marble mantel by surmounting it with a stunning work of art flanked with a pair of elegant Japanese vases. Make a country bedroom fireplace even cozier by topping it with a display of favorite plates or painted platters. Or top a sleek modern fireplace with an overscale starburst mirror and place an asymmetrical arrangement of tall ceramic pots to one side.

If your fireplace can use an upgrade, change its surround or mantel to elevate its stature or tweak its character altogether. A few thoughtful architectural details can turn a bland room into a grand room. You might top a fireplace that lacks a mantel with a sleek wall-mounted floating shelf. Or you could brighten a dingy brick fireplace by painting it white. You could also create a sense of substance around a small fireplace by flanking it with built-in or ready-made bookshelves.

The fireplace opening also offers an opportunity for creativity. Fill it with a fluffy potted fern, a large basket of dried

Casually placed picture frames, votive candles and outdoor gear look right at home atop the rough-hewn mantel of this rustic fireplace.

hydrangeas, a collection of pillar candles or a bundle of birch logs. Fireplace screens and accoutrements, such as shovels and pokers, offer additional options for enriching the character of your fireplace with crafted touches and personal style. Consider these fresh approaches to turning a fireplace into a gracious focal point.

Picture perfect Nine tiny framed images flanked by a pair of topiaries offer a whimsical focal point over a casual white-painted brick fireplace *(top, left)*. A simple painted fire screen adds an appropriate finishing touch.

Casual attire For a casual room, an all-white mantel and chimney breast keep the room crisp and provide a perfect backdrop for accents that can be changed seasonally *(top, center)*. Complement the relaxed spirit of the space by topping the mantel with a watercolor painted by a family member, or an unframed folk art flea-market find. For a cottage feel, flank the art with a trio of ironstone (or other kinds of white ceramic) pitchers brimming with picks from your garden. Add more color with a flower-filled basket or galvanized bucket in front of the hearth—and fill the fireplace with artfully arranged sculptural pieces of driftwood.

A warm hearth In this transitional-style setting *(top, right)*, traditional-style accents with a contemporary twist contribute to an appealing tableau. In lieu of a botanical print, a large-scale black-and-white photo or lithograph of a tree or flower in a crisp frame can add zip with modern edge to the scene. Instead of centering the artwork on the wall and flanking it with candleholders, rest it on one side of the mantel and set it off with a pair of pillar candles in streamlined hurricane lamps on the other to mix proportions. Choose a fresh, sunny paint color for the wall behind the mantel for a note of updated warmth.

Vintage style A brick-front fireplace works in tandem with a plank-paneled wall and old-timey travel poster to create a balanced vignette in character with an unpretentious cottage *(bottom, right)*. Painting the paneling an antique white gives the poster's walnut-stained frame and the floor added presence. A well-edited collection of accents perfects the vintage style.

CURB APPEAL

Whether your home's facade will be seen for the first time by a prospective buyer coming to take a look, or again and again by family and friends visiting a home you plan to keep for the rest of your life, you'll want it to look its very best the moment it comes into view. Ultimately, the landscape, driveway, walking path or stairs that lead to your home should be cultivated, pruned, shaped and placed to frame your house in a way that shows it off as a focal point in its own right.

Just as the interior spaces of your home need to be tidy and thoughtfully laid out, your home's exterior should also be well-preserved and its windows squeaky clean. The least any potential buyer will expect in a home is a roof in good condition and solid siding or walls. So, assuming your home's foundation is solid, its roof is leak-free, and its siding or walls are well-maintained, turn your attention toward the easy ways you can brighten the exterior of your home, enabling it to intimate the inviting haven within.

Keeping It Clean

Your first step is to give patios, decks, porches and terraces a thoroughly clean sweep. If concrete floors, walkways, driveways, and wood or vinyl siding are in need of cleaning, consider renting a pressure cleaner, which sprays a jet of water over surfaces to rinse stains, grime and dirt away. You can rent one from an equipment renter, or call a cleaning service to handle it for you. Either way, you should be able to clean an entire house, drive and deck in half a day. Before you use a pressure cleaner on siding, however, test it out on a small area to be sure it doesn't cause any damage or abrade a paint job.

Pressure washers don't work on windows, however, so to get those clean you'll need to rely on a bucket of water and cleaning liquid, a squeegee and a lint-free cloth. The other option is to call a professional window cleaning service. Go with a national franchise or contact a local company with a good reputation or one that's been referred by someone you trust. Be sure to choose someone who is bonded, licensed and insured. And never clean windows in direct sunlight or streaks will appear.

Cultivating the Landscape

The lawn, trees, shrubs and gardens surrounding your home play a strong supporting role in the impression your home gives. For a home you plan to sell, an appealing first impression can either make or break a deal.

Even if you don't have a green thumb, you can establish the foundation of a vibrant landscape by investing at least $2,000 or

TOP: A slate path and steps lead to an inviting front door topped with a pediment and flanked with sidelights and pretty planters.

BOTTOM: Surrounded by the classic picket fence laced with pretty white pansies, this little house looks like the ultimate "home, sweet home."

$3,000 in sod, flower beds trimmed with brick edging, a few shrubs and trees, and modest plantings. If you plan to sell your home and the landscape needs attention, keep in mind that you're developing the yard to showcase the house and shouldn't invest in longer-term landscape improvements. If you're fortunate enough to have the funds to enlist a gardener, however, then urge this person to address any of the common landscaping problems that can nix the sale of your home, such as drainage problems that create water seepage in a basement or crawl space, poor grading (your yard should slope away from your house at least one inch for eight feet of lawn), trees that are too close to the house, damaged underground sprinkler systems, and unstable earth that can cause problems. Naturally, if you plan to keep your home, you'd want any issues in these areas resolved for your long-term comfort, too.

If your essential groundwork has already been done, however, then your job is to maintain your landscape by regularly mowing the lawn, trimming shrubs, tending flowers and pruning trees. Then you can move on to some of the cosmetic touches that give your patio, deck, lawn and gardens personality and curb appeal. For example, as more and more eating and living spaces move toward the outdoors, various soft furnishings make these spaces almost as comfortable as their interior counterparts. Chair pads, lounge chair cushions and tablecloths add comfort and style to an outdoor setting. But other elements, such as umbrellas, canopies, awnings and cabanas, can actually define an outdoor living space. Also, window treatments, including floor-length draperies along a portico or roll-up shades in the windows of a screened-in porch, control light during the day or provide privacy at night. For soft furnishings that are intended for outdoor or indoor/outdoor use, choose fabrics that can withstand the rigors of the elements, including dirt, harsh sunlight and rain.

Potted plants or topiaries, window boxes, pergolas and arbors are other simple additions to brighten a landscape or front entrance with cultivated touches of natural beauty. If gardening doesn't come to you easily, choose low-maintenance plants. For the greatest chances for success, always choose flowers and shrubs that are native to your area.

Lighting is another element that can make your outdoor spaces prettier and more functional. If you plan to keep your home, consider integrated landscape lighting to highlight trees and walkways at night. Lovely sconces and lanterns at the front door accentuate the entrance and add to the beauty of your home's facade. Hurricane lamps and paper lanterns are great for entertaining outdoors in the evening. And strings of lights wrapped around tree branches, votives, tabletop lanterns and other outdoor luminaries can serve as seasonal brighteners.

COST-EFFECTIVE UPGRADES

If you're going to invest in an exterior upgrade, consider these tips that will offer you a good return on your investment:

- Architectural asphalt shingles improve heat efficiency.
- Gray slate pavers create an upscale look on a walkway and front steps.
- Sidelights and a transom around a front door bring light into an entrance hall or foyer.
- Install dormers to add eye-catching appeal and introduce additional interior light, space and ventilation.
- Plant vines that grow up the sides of your home to visually expand its dimensions, and introduce low-growing plants around your home to ground it.
- Install substantial hardware in a unified finish—door handles and knockers, house numbers, and mailboxes—for a polished appearance.
- Replace or pressure-clean worn or damaged aluminum, vinyl, wood or brick siding. The return on investment in most parts of the country is 100 percent or more.

The floaty white canvas panels soften an arched passageway between a dining room and loggia. Metal hooks hold the fabric back to let in sunlight.

ADD CURB APPEAL

Paint the front door an engaging color, such as a rich red or bright blue, but be sure it complements its surroundings.

Dress up the front door with seasonal embellishments Use floral swags or wreaths to celebrate spring, the fall harvest or winter holidays.

Parade a series of real or faux topiaries in a front hall window They will bring a lively touch of the outdoors to the indoor space.

Treat the front stoop or porch as if it were a room Flower arrangements or potted plants, a bench, a charming door knocker and the glow of a pair of sconces seen from the curb can make visitors feel welcome before they even reach the door.

Add privacy without losing a key source of natural light Install frosted glass etched with an eye-catching design in sidelights flanking a front door.

Update an old or dented storm/ screen door combination with a new, more energy-efficient—and more attractive—style.

Mount draperies on crane rods behind a windowed entry door Adjust the rod to provide appropriate amounts of light and privacy.

Lay down a welcome mat Whether it's a seasonal image, monogrammed or basic coir mat, make sure to provide a place where guests can wipe the outdoor grit and grime off their shoes. Replace worn or dirty mats regularly.

Rows of potted trees or plants define spaces that lack fences.

TOP: Surrounded by flowering shrubs and a pristine lawn, this red shingle house in the Berkshires exudes warmth and comfort.

BOTTOM, LEFT: A cutting garden provides an ever-changing display of blossoms from season to season.

BOTTOM, RIGHT: A mix of low-maintenance plants keeps the yard of this California house looking lush.

ABOVE, LEFT:
Slipcovered chairs, a
full-length tablecloth
and a folding screen turn
a backyard patio into a
cozy indoor/outdoor
setting.

ABOVE, RIGHT:
Surrounded by flowing
sheer curtains, a
homemade dining
table and bench on a
front porch is the ideal
spot for an impromptu
summer picnic

LEFT: Sofas and
chairs with cushions
upholstered in durable
indoor-outdoor fabrics
can sit outside all year.

RIGHT: Cushioned wicker
and rattan pieces are
classics on a covered
verandah.

QUICK FIXES

INSTANT ART Create your own art in no time by surrounding scraps of wrapping paper, wallcovering or even fabric remnants with a mix of different frames in various sizes but matching colors for a harmonious assemblage.

HERE COMES THE SUN Brighten the dreariest day with a classic sun face like this one. All you'll need to make your own is a bit of cement and the right mold. Rub whitewash on the finished piece with cheesecloth to give it a pretty patina.

STEP IT UP Personalize your garden with homemade stepping stones cast from cement. Craft just one to add a jaunty touch in front of a flower bed, or create several with fun designs—like this perky dragonfly—to forge a path to a pool or garden shed.

PARTY TIME Set the scene for a perfect outdoor summer fête. Clip fresh blossoms from the garden and set them in drinking glasses or bud vases at each place setting. Cover cushions with fabrics in lively patterns and happy colors. Stow linens in baskets on a charming vintage étagère. Scent the air with pots of fragrant herbs or lavender. Craft a napkin caddy and give embroidered napkins as gifts. Fill an overscale urn with ice, wine and champagne, pop the corks and let the party begin!

Acknowledgements

The talent and energy of several people went into the making of this book and all deserve our acknowledgement and thanks. Much of the information contained in these pages was gleaned through reporting done by several staff editors and regular contributors to the Woman's Day Special Interest Publications, including Pamela Acuff, Bernadette Baczynski, Megan Fulweiler, Maryjane Fromm, Nancy Herrick, Judi Ketteler Katie Kretschmer, Allison Lind, Ayn-Monique Tetreault-Rooney Klahrer, and William Weathersby Jr.

Many designers and architects have shared their wisdom and work for this book, including Rachel Ashwell, Keith Baltimore, Kitty Bartholomew, Ellen Baron-Goldstein, Kathryn Eileen Boyd, Jennifer Blume, Barclay Butera, Nels Christianson, Mark Christofi, Lori Dennis, Jamie Drake, Donna Dufresne, Ray Ehscheid, Dena Fishbein, Jessica Helgerson, Jackie Higgins, Roman Kujawa, Jeannette Kyser, Libby Langdon, Greg Lanza, Judith Lattuca, Anne Lombardi-Rohrberg, Victoria Lyon, Saverio Mancina, Will McGall, Art McShane, Kathy Monkman, Marie Moss, Katy Naghavi, Nora Napientek, Stephanie Nigro, Christopher Peacock, Mary Randelman, Marilyn Rose, Joe Ruggiero, Nestor Santa-Cruz, Susan Sargent, Annie Selke, Kate Singer, Jaclyn Smith, Laurie Smith, Audrey Soldau, Patricia Stadel, Irwin Weiner, Michael Wilkinson and Vern Yip.

And a number of stylists have contributed to much of the visual content in these pages, including Sarah Alba, Darra Baker, Michelle Bignell, Lindsey Buchleitner, Susan Burns, Andrea Caughey, Lori Dennis, Gridley & Graves, Heidi Hamilton, Sunday Hendrickson, Sheryl Ketner, Laurent Laborie, Audrey Lee, Ingrid Leess, Nicola Marc, Lisa McGee, Marie Moss, Arden Nelson, Dan Pasky, Donna Pizzi, Ellie Roper, Hillary Rose, Gisela Rose, Jay Spratt, Larry Stanley, Jeff Styles, Lynda Sutton, Donna Talley, Erinn Valencich and Ruth Ellen Wells. We are grateful to all.

Special thanks also go to Matthew Levinson, Jennifer Ko and Anthi Keeling for their production assistance.

Finally, our gratitude goes to Dorothée Walliser for developing the original idea for this book and shepherding it through its development and publication.

Resources

American Home Furnishing Alliance (ahfa.us)
Armstrong (armstrong.com)
AsktheBuilder (AsktheBuilder.com)
Beach Glass Interior Design (beachglassinteriordesign.com)
Baker (kohlerinteriors.com)
Ballard Designs (ballarddesigns.com)
Bed, Bath & Beyond (bedbathandbeyond.com)
Broyhill (broyhillfurniture.com)
Budget Blinds (budgetblinds.com
CaesarStone (caesarstoneus.com)
Calico Corners (calicocorners.com)
California Closets (californiaclosets.com)
Carpet and Rug Institute (carpet-rug.org)
Ceramic Tile Distributors Association (ctdahome.org)
Christianson Lee Studios (christiansonlee.com)
ClosetMaid (closetmaid.com)
Container Store, The (containerstore.com)
Contrast Design Group (contrastdesigngroup.com)
Costco (costco.com)
Country Curtains (countrycurtains.com)
Crack Team, The (thecrackteam.com)
David-Michael Design, Inc. (david-michael.net)
Direct Buy (directbuy.com)
Dunis Studios (dunisstudios.com)
Eclipse by Vinylbuilt (eclipseshutters.com)
Exciting Windows (excitingwindows.com)
Ez A Peel (ezapeel.com)
Flexi-Wall (flexiwall.com)
For Life Products (forlifeproducts.com)
Fypon (fypon.com)
Gaiam (gaiam.com)
Garnet Hill (garnethill.com)
Great Windows (greatwindows.com)
Gulfcoast's (homedepot.com)
Hartzstone (hartzstone.com)
Home Depot (homedepot.com)
ICI Paints (icipaints.com)
Ikea (ikea.com)
JC Penney (jcp.com)
Kate Singer Home (katesingerhome.com)
Lands' End (landsend.com)
La-Z-Boy (la-z-boy.com)
Lee Industries (leeindustries.com)
Lowe's (lowes.com)
Lysol (lysol.com)
Macbeth Collection (themacbethcollection.com)
Millbrook Custom Kitchens (millbrookkitchens.com)
Miracle Method (miraclemethod.com)
Mr. Clean (mrclean.com)
National Guild of Professional Paperhangers (ngpp.org)
Nextten's Floor Revive (nextten.com)
North Prairie Tileworks (handmadetile.com)
Organize It (organzeit.com)
Philadelphia Shutter Company, The (philadelphiashutters.com)
PointClickHome (pointclickhome.com)
Pottery Barn (potterybarn.com)
Quick Step (quick-step.com)
Razvi Design Studio, Inc. (razvidesign.com)
Real Milk Paint Co., The (realmilkpaint.com)
Restoration Hardware (restorationhardware.com)
Room Service Home (roomservicehome.com)
Rowe Furniture (rowefurniture.com)
Sam's Club (samsclub.com)
Scotch-Gard (3m.com)
Seabrook (seabrookwallpaper.com)
Sherwin-Williams (sherwin-williams.com)
Shoebby (shoebby.com)
Shutterland (shutterland.com)
Silestone (sliestoneusa.com)
Stewart Allen (707-431-2116)
Lutron Electronics (lutron.com)
Smith & Noble (smithandnoble.com)
StyleMark (fypon.com)
Sunburst Shutters (sunburstshutters.com)
Sure Fit (surefit.net)
Thibaut (thibautdesign.com)
Tile Council of North America's Web (Tileusa.com) and National Tile Contractors Association (tile-assn.com)
Walker Zanger (walkerznager.com)
Waverly (waverly.com)
Wilsonart (wilsonart.com)
World Floor Covering Association (wfca.org)
York (yorkwall.com)